UNBOUND
An Immigrant Daughter's Journey of Reckoning, Unraveling Shame, and Reclaiming Her Worth

SERENA ARORA

LANDON
HAIL
PRESS

Copyright© 2025 Serena Arora
All Rights Reserved

This book or any portion thereof may not be reproduced or used in any manner without the express written permission of the publisher, except for the use of brief quotations in a book review.

Paperback ISBN: 978-1-959955-72-6
Hardback ISBN: 978-1-959955-73-3

Cover design by Serena Arora, Rich Johnson, Spectacle Photo
Cover photo by Jesse Littlebird, JesseLittlebird.com
Published by Landon Hail Press
www.serenaarora.com

Although the author and publisher have made every effort to ensure the accuracy and completeness of information contained in this book, we assume no responsibility for errors, inaccuracies, omissions, or any inconsistency herein. Any slights on people, places, or organizations are unintentional. Some names and details have been changed for privacy purposes. The material in this book is provided for educational purposes only. No responsibility for loss occasioned to any person or corporate body acting or refraining to act as a result of reading material in this book can be accepted by the author or publisher.

This book is dedicated to my Chinese mother, the bound-footed women who came before her, and the girls whose unbound feet inherited the privilege to walk in their shoes.

Testimonials

"This book was healing, cathartic, and deeply resonant. Serena's honesty and introspection drew me in from the very first page. I saw so much of my own journey reflected in hers. The way she shares her experiences with love, seeking validation, cultural identity, and healing generational wounds is powerful and relatable. It had me reflecting on my own upbringing in ways I hadn't before. Her story is a mirror, an invitation, and a gift. It deserves a place on every bookshelf."
—Pia Edberg, author & book doula

"*Unbound* is inspiring, uplifting, and refreshingly honest! Everyone only wants to show the shiny parts, but Serena takes us right into this deepest, darkest, messiest of truths, reminding us that claiming your worth, power, and dignity starts within. *Unbound* will remind you that you have been fierce and free all along the way."
—Julia Hausch, osteopath

"Amongst the top most visceral moments I had while reading a book, it felt like a journey of forgiveness. Playing small, intergenerational trauma, pattern recognition, and criticism are all part of my story, as well. Watching Serena unravel and connect the through-lines of her journey inspired me to find some grace for myself in mine."
—Christina Michael, holistic business consultant

"Serena has such a unique and gifted way of making her feelings of being different and out of place, as a young girl and teenager, so identifiable. Beautifully written and engaging, these are the stories I want to read about—strong, creative women facing life challenges, inspiring me to have more compassion for my mom, carve out my own path, and stand on my own two feet."

—Vicky Kravariotis, teacher & flight attendant

"Wow! What an incredible book, story, and life! The author takes readers on a deeply personal and transformative journey, reinventing herself time and time again in the ongoing search for peace and a place to call home. Her storytelling is poignant and profound—raw in its honesty, and yet so beautifully relatable. With themes of identity, belonging, and resilience, the book shines a light on the experience of growing up as a second-generation immigrant. The emotional complexity of guilt, grit, and the pressure to fit in is captured with both nuance and heart. This is a book that will especially resonate with young women who have ever felt like outsiders. It offers a mirror for some and a window for others—and above all, a message of empowerment. You'll finish this book feeling inspired, seen, and already hoping the author has another one on the way."

—Monique Giroux, bestselling author & coach

Contents

Testimonials _____ v
Foreword _____ 1
Introduction _____ 5
Chapter 1: DON'T WASTE THE PRETTY _____ 10
Chapter 2: IMMIGRIT _____ 24
Chapter 3: BUSTER BROWN _____ 52
Chapter 4: PAKI _____ 62
Chapter 5: WHORES & PROSTITUTES _____ 72
Chapter 6: WINONA _____ 79
Chapter 7: WRONG SIDE OF THE TRACKS _____ 93
Chapter 8: CRAB FOR LUNCH _____ 105
Chapter 9: ASIA, AUZ, AND CANCER _____ 110
Chapter 10: GOD, GIVE ME A SIGN _____ 117
Chapter 11: GOODBYE, SERENA _____ 125
Chapter 12: FIRST MARRIAGE PROPOSAL _____ 139
Chapter 13: LAND OF ENTRAPMENT _____ 152
Chapter 14: OUT OF GAS _____ 163
Chapter 15: CAASAA SOMBRIIIA _____ 171
Chapter 16: RAVISHED _____ 178

Chapter 17: YOU CAN'T ALWAYS GET WHAT YOU
    WANT _____ 193
Chapter 18: SECOND MARRIAGE PROPOSAL _____ 208
Chapter 19: HONEY, I'M HOME _____ 224
Acknowledgments _____ 240
About the Author _____ 242

Foreword

IN ANY GIVEN LIFETIME, the journey of the soul is long and winding, one that includes many strides forward, frequent backsliding, and side forays down unmarked trails. The soul's migration is always toward a sense of home, a sense of belonging. Along the way, we all must reconcile the fundamental splits that tear at our hearts and minds.

On the long journey, we sometimes feel elevated and free, and other times trapped and stranded. Over the course of a lifetime, some simply get stuck in survival mode. Through much trial and error, and after traipsing across many lonely highways and feeling the sting of lost love, we may land, if fortunate, in a haven of peace inside.

For those willing to undertake the serpentine pilgrimage toward wholeness and belonging, courage and fortitude are necessary. For there is no exact map or compass, no GPS to locate yourself along the way. For each of us, our quest is unique, particular to you, a travel that has never been undertaken in the exact way that yours must be followed and pursued. For this reason, each of us needs some combination of the following: perseverance, a sense of underlying trust, deep longing, and faith. Faith may be most important, yet most tricky to come by. Like courage, faith has no formula, no satellite coordinates to go by. And faith, by necessity, is beyond reason. On the path, faith is like a headlamp cast forth into the great unknown.

The journey of the soul requires navigating the complex weave of karma that we inherit from "previous lives" — from our ancestors, culture, and country of origin. Karma includes the many diverse threads within a family history, each with its own strivings, beliefs, agendas, hopes, and fears. While this migration is jumbled and bewildering for us all, it is especially complex for second-generation immigrants, born onto a soil that may be thousands of miles away from their parents' home country. In a world that has recently witnessed massive global migration, this experience is relevant to so many today. It inevitably includes hauling around a heavy backpack full of the first-generation parents' hopes and dreams.

This experience is a threshold experience, at the edge of two worlds, where the wayfarer is neither of the old world left behind nor of the new world that lies ahead. It is here that we encounter the raw, beautiful and tender tale of personal transformation and discovery, *Unbound: An Immigrant Daughter's Journey of Reckoning, Unraveling Shame, and Reclaiming Her Worth*. At once a deeply personal odyssey of self-discovery, it speaks to the transpersonal — the global trial, taken by so many in the quest for safety, security, wholeness, and belonging.

In the world of trauma, it is said that the wound is the greatest healer. The rupture involved in migration, leaving behind one's cultural heritage and ancestral ties and moving to a strange and foreign land, holds both promise and pain in the opportunity for self-renewal. It is no surprise then that the children of immigrants harbor feelings of both loyalty and disloyalty to their family of origins. For the new second-generation of immigrant travelers, the question is always, where to place allegiance? Cast into an unfamiliar landscape, the children of immigrant parents find themselves left to forge their own identity. It is the remake of identity that we turn to in these pages.

On the path to wholeness and embodiment, each of us endures a kind of rite of passage. We must stretch beyond the confines of the familiar and beyond the expectations and presuppositions of our family of origin. This path of discovery is like the practice of yoga—stretching, pushing, reaching, and expanding outside the parameters of who we think we are and who we think we ought to be. We open ourselves up to something that, at first, felt unimaginable and beyond our grasp. Little by little, we come to embody a new sense of belonging. We come to embody a newfound sense of self. By altering the energetic matrix of our cells, we come to occupy a sense of greater coherence inside.

This process of transformation is not limited to physical transformation. On the steps toward wholeness, reflection, remembrance, and meditation are invaluable. Via the help of guiding angels—therapists, coaches, dream workers, and modern-day shamans—we come to identify the command of internalized voices.

In her poem "The Journey," the poet Mary Oliver wrote of the old voices, "'Mend my life,' each voice cried." Over time, we learn to parse our own voice from the voices of expectation and want that may go back generations. Some of these voices may be encouraging and instructive, while others are critical, suspicious, and intrusive. Undoubtedly, these soundless voices have sway over the spin of our thoughts and the beating of our heart.

The walk toward wholeness requires feeling into the wounds we carry—some inherited, some accumulated in this lifetime. In time, we learn not to duck and cover from our pain or simply to project our pain outward, but to come to acknowledge it, to feel it, and to come to befriend our "pain body."

The path to healing requires acknowledging that we each have a multi-layered and messy karmic history. It is the very act of embracing the complexity of our personal history that gives way to self-acceptance. When we come to accept our signature history together, with its losses, wounds, and scars, we heal the ache and pangs of our wounded heart. This acceptance is the very seed for compassionate presence and non-judgmental awareness. We realize that all beings down through the generations have had to navigate the intricate weave of a familial history.

All readers will recognize strands of their own life in the pages that follow on the journey from the small, fretful, ambiguous self toward a bigger, wider, and more loving self. Here we can relate to the wrenching gut feeling of first being bound by circumstance, only to discover in time that we have become who we were born to be. With faith and diligence on the path of practice, may we each discover for ourselves, in our own way, the fullest expression of our unbound soul.

Tias Little
Santa Fe, New Mexico
Author of *Yoga of the Subtle Body*

Introduction

I LINKED MY ELBOW under my eighty-five-year-old mother's arm and grabbed her bony hand. She gripped the railing tightly with the other as I helped her slowly climb the stairs. Carefully placing one foot in front of the next, she was one step closer to her safe haven—her bedroom—the only place she said still, "I feel like myself."

Parkinson's was ravaging her body while dementia devoured her brain, and with each step, I couldn't help but wonder if she'd still remember who I was, the next time I came back to see her.

Living halfway across the world from aging parents is certainly a challenge, but one I'm accustomed to. I've straddled two worlds my entire life: I'm a Western-born daughter to Eastern immigrant parents, half-Chinese and half-Indian, formally educated in both French and English, who juggled two careers at one time, moved every few years, and lived away from my family my entire adult life.

My mother's disease has affected our immediate family—my dad, my older sister, and myself—all in different ways. While the natural caregiver side of me understands my mother in ways the other two just don't, the daughter-duty side of me is grieving the loss of a mother I've known my whole life. It is a sad, tender process to say goodbye to a mom who may or may not recognize me the next time I see her.

Since our family travels so often, we don't typically cry when we say goodbye. This time, however, as my mom and I stood at the threshold of her bedroom, saying goodnight for the last time before I left to return to my home in Costa Rica, I couldn't hold back.

My Chinese mother's tiny 4'8", seventy-five-pound frame exuded the strength of a lioness as she looked into my tear-streaked face. She turned to face me, her small Asian eyes wildly mirroring mine, and whispered softly, "Be brave."

Forcing a smile through the tears, I whispered back, "I get that from you, Mom."

My mom is warrior exemplified—independent, fierce, resilient. In all my fifty years of life, I have never seen my mother cry. She's the poster child for the adage "tiny but mighty." She birthed two babies by C-section in her late thirties, had tumors removed from her colon and breast, survived a World War, cancer, several broken bones, and is now fighting her way through Parkinson's and dementia.

With each fight, my mom cultivated yet another level of courage that transcended the fear from her past, accumulating armor over eight decades until she would eventually find herself trapped inside her own sheer rigidity.

"I love you, Mom," I said.

"I love you, too, Serena," she replied with a certainty and assuredness I hadn't heard from her before, on those rare occasions when she'd say those three elusive words out loud.

Growing up in an Asian immigrant family, saying and hearing "I love you" just didn't occur. Love was implied, and attempting to articulate your emotions fell on deaf ears. My parents grew up during World War II, so to expect them to hold anything more than what they already had to give was unthinkable. Thus, this level of embodied wisdom was simply not modeled for me. Invisible rules and traditions were imposed instead: don't be too emotional, too vulnerable, too passionate, too expressive, too complacent, too loud, or too anything, if you know what's good for you. I call this *immigrit*.

Immigrit gifted me with the ability to create so many incredible opportunities for myself and others. And while it taught me relentless work ethic, strong morals, and striking resilience, it also chipped away at my confidence, self-worth, and true feminine essence.

As a daughter of immigrants, I was expected to succeed at all costs, and yet I constantly felt I was failing miserably at it all. Any feminine nourishment I needed, in order to grow, was replaced with unsolicited advice that wasn't to be questioned. If I dared play by another set of rules—namely my own—I would feel judged, criticized, or outright rejected. I call this *immiguilt*.

I felt guilty for not playing by my parents' traditions and rules, for following my own intuition, and for being too big to fit into my immigrant parents' narrow comfort zone. My being denied the opportunity to practice standing for what I believed and truly desired led to my doubting myself at every turn.

I learned that it was safer to play small, to trust others' opinions rather than my own, and that failure was never an option. As my self-doubt grew, my deep insecurity drove my decisions to seek external validation, to feel afraid of failure, and to stay hidden behind a fear and shame that wasn't even mine.

This is that story.

My mom asked me to not publish this book until she passes, so as not to "air our dirty laundry." As I see it, this is the exact reason *why* I wrote this book: for and because of her. I'm telling my story to give voice to those who are tethered to their past and stuck in the silence of the culture gap.

Writing and publishing this book is itself breaking a generational pattern that blazes a trail for my niece and nephew and so many others, inviting them to step into unfamiliar territory of breaking a generational pattern of guilt (immiguilt) and speaking the vulnerable truth with confidence and pride. I'm telling my story so it doesn't become their story or any other young girl's story, as she navigates her own pathway to womanhood. I'm telling my story to reconcile my relationship to daughter-duty.

I see so much of myself in my mom and wouldn't be the woman I am today had it not been for her. While we're painfully similar, I'm also aware that, in order to not fully follow in her footsteps, I must break the patterns that bind me to the misinformed lineage of our past. One particular pattern is loyalty. To her, loyalty means conservatively following in the safe footsteps of those who walked before her, learning from their mistakes, following their rules, and carefully treading through life.

To me, loyalty means being brave enough to build a bridge and stand on it alone. To risk breaking away from the fear that lives in my lineage, and blazing a newly informed trail for those who walk behind me. As a daughter, sister, auntie, and stepmom, I believe it's my daughter-duty to interrupt outdated family patterns and change the trajectory of our future, empowering the next generation to meet me fearlessly on the bridge.

Hence the publication of this book while my mom is still alive. This book is my roadmap to getting to that bridge. May it be a guide for all women to unearth their own powerful feminine presence buried underneath the fear and shame. May it be a catalyst to set raw, vulnerable daughter-duty conversations in motion. May it give us all permission to unabashedly feel, as feeling is the cornerstone of humanity itself.

Each chapter begins with a pivotal moment in my life, a raw and real memory of when my insecurity stood in my way, bowled me over, or stopped me in my tracks. In these pages, I take you back to the first time I met doubt—at only four years old. I share my own teenage struggles with shame to remind you you're not alone. And I untangle my self-inflicted binding to reveal an unbound freedom within. But that isn't the end of the story. It's just the beginning. Because the road to enoughness is a long, arduous one.

So, buckle up, my friend.

And above all, "Be brave."

Chapter 1

DON'T WASTE THE PRETTY

IT WAS OCTOBER 2011. I gazed at the open road ahead, watching it stretch endlessly toward a saffron-hued sky. I was driving nearly three hours to *the city*, as it was referred to by the local residents of the small northern lake town where I lived. I toggled the volume button on my car stereo, listening intently to the voices coming through the speakers.

Arielle Ford and Katherine Woodward Thomas were deep in conversation about relationships on *The Art of Love* webinar. I was thirty-seven years old, and it was the first time I had signed up for anything like this, hoping to find some answers about my own deteriorating marriage.

I glanced at the dashboard clock and sighed, whispering to myself, "One more hour to go." Instinctively, I pressed down on the gas pedal, gripped the steering wheel a little tighter, and fixed my eyes on the horizon, as though they could will *the city* to magically appear sooner. It didn't.

This trip to the provincial capital city of Edmonton from that lake town was a 130-mile stretch of single-lane highway, lined with farmers' golden fields dotted with giant, round hay bales, random homes, dilapidated barns, and oversized red stop signs. The growing number of stop signs signaled I was getting closer to the city.

Lately, I had been driving this familiar route alone, so, in order to pass the time, I played little games with myself. I'd time out how long it took between stop signs, feeling accomplished if I was just one second faster than the last. I watched the fields whip by, squinting until they dissolved into an infinite golden blur.

This reminded me of the sensation I'd had as a kid, riding the Polar Express, a fast-spinning ride at the renowned ten-day exhibition and rodeo in my hometown, The Calgary Stampede. The Polar Express was an assault to the senses, a combination of fear and pure exhilaration while music blared. The ride sped up whenever the DJ got people to scream louder. I felt an intoxicating thrill throughout my entire body as my light frame hovered dangerously over the seat and I hung on for dear life.

I was born and raised in Calgary in the seventies and eighties, and I left when I was seventeen. Despite never returning there to live permanently, it is still the city I call "home." After high school, I moved to Edmonton for university and then even farther north, to that small town on the lake for my first French immersion teaching job in 1996.

I was a feisty, bright-eyed, half-Chinese, half-Indian, twenty-one-year-old city girl with no idea what northern small-town life would be like, but I soon found out. Excited to start my budding teaching career and experience new challenges in a new place to live, I also quickly realized I didn't quite fit in. While I'd moved only six hours north of Calgary, my culture shock living in that little town on the lake was palpable.

SERENA ARORA

There were as many people in my high school as in that little town at the time. My perspectives, experiences, values, and ideals proved very different from those of the local residents. At twenty-one, I had already traveled farther and visited more places in the world than many of the older townspeople in their entire lives. I was one of only four Asians living there at the time. I wasn't planning on having children. And only a handful of the locals had heard of yoga, quinoa, or spirulina. Needless to say, I ended up making many trips to *the city*.

Each time I drove those remote northern highways, the rhythmic thrum of my tires against the asphalt seemed to echo the pulse of my inner conflict. I found myself caught between two worlds: the one I'd been born into, where my parents' diverse culture and traditions had long dictated the rules; and the other that was going to be mine to define during what ended up being fifteen years of living in that little town on the lake, off and on.

I had driven those highways so often, I could have done it with my eyes closed. And, to their detriment, some people did. Those northern Alberta roads were infamous for their harsh winter road conditions, big-game wildlife, nightfall by 4:00 p.m. in winter, and a growing number of tired, possibly hungover oil rig workers rushing to and from their shifts. So, while driving those roads with your eyes closed was a real possibility, it could also easily be the death of you.

In fact, one stretch of that northern highway was even dubbed "Death Road." So why was I still driving those roads? I had met a guy in that little northern town on the lake, Nate. Over the span of sixteen years, Nate went from being a guy I had met to my longtime, long-distance boyfriend and finally, to my husband. And just like that, those remote northern highways became the backdrop for the first half of my adult life.

Nate and I had an instant connection. I felt light, joyful, and free to be myself when I was with him. He was the complete opposite of anything I was used to during my rigid upbringing and immigrant family life. Things between us felt real and authentic from the start, and, boy, did we ever laugh. Nate was funny. Like, *really* funny. Not just lighthearted funny, though there was that, too; he had the one-liner wit and timing of a skilled comedian. Whenever Nate was around, there was no shortage of ear-to-ear smiles, bellyaching laughs, silent snorts, and unrestrained guffaws. Even the haters couldn't stifle their chuckles.

Nate and I were both young teachers in our twenties who enjoyed nature, food, family, and summer vacations. Things just seemed relaxed, carefree, and easy with us—something undeniably foreign to me and my serious Asian upbringing. He'd often parrot to me, "Okaaaay, city slicker, don't sweat the small stuff!" And I found it refreshing.

As we got to know each other, I also noticed Nate's natural ability to ground me. I would literally fall asleep in his lap after work some days, waking up in a pool of drool spilling over the side of my cheek, onto his shoulder, and down the back of his shirt. He didn't seem to mind. In fact, Nate didn't seem to mind much of anything. He was as easy going as they came: a superb athlete, humble, and one of the most compassionate people I'd ever met. The only thing he made sure of in life was that he didn't take it too seriously.

While Nate and I were both teachers, we were otherwise from two very different worlds in almost every way. Me, a petite, brown, mixed-race, Canadian-born, naïve city girl, who found herself drowning in the inconveniences and culture shock of small-town living. And he, a burly, White, small-town farm boy, who found himself swept up by a small, Asian whirlwind who stormed into his northern hometown on the lake one summer day in 1996.

While nothing seemed to bother Nate, which could be considered a good thing, most everything seemed overly serious to me. Here's the thing: you can take the girl out of her rigid immigrant family environment, but you can't completely take the rigid immigrant family environment out of the girl. I still cared too much about social graces and grammar, scrutinized work ethic and finances, and held fast to lofty professional goals, travel, personal growth, and success. I inherently *sweat the small stuff*.

Nate, with his deep-rooted connections to the land and community, was the very embodiment of the simple life I hadn't known existed. His world felt foreign to me, yet I was drawn to it. Meanwhile, my own upbringing—the expectations, the social rules, the pressure to "succeed"—left me torn between fitting in and standing out, between living up to the expectations of my family and forging my own path.

The culture gap between me and Nate was wide. So, over the years, the carefree attitude I had found so appealing at first became a pain point in our relationship. And after fifteen years of differing priorities, we started to drive down separate lanes and then divergent highways, until we were headed in opposite directions toward two completely different places.

Feeling deeply conflicted in our not-so-serious yet very serious relationship and marriage, I did the only thing a conditioned daughter of immigrants knew to do—I ignored it and immersed myself in my work, my environment, and my community. I taught over forty yoga classes each week in my studio or at schools, colleges, senior facilities, gyms, and community centers. I hosted and led special events, workshops, meetings, and conferences. I spearheaded a grassroots environmental group, offering documentary film screenings and radio interviews. I taught violin lessons, produced yoga DVDs, and collaborated with other artisans, healthcare providers, and healers.

It was a lot. I worked a lot, drank a lot, and was around a lot of people a lot of the time. Everyone except Nate.

While I poured myself into everything and everyone else, we still managed to eat dinner together some evenings (a meal Nate would generously prepare while I finished up the last class of the evening in my studio). But instead of talking and connecting, we often ate dinner side-by-side on the couch while watching prerecorded episodes of reality TV. After a while, Nate and I became ships passing in the night. We stopped having conversations, we stopped having fun together, and worse, we stopped laughing.

By avoiding the hard conversations in my marriage, I felt disconnected and disheartened. Sadly, I was no stranger to that pattern and those feelings. I had grown up observing my immigrant parents' marriage and, after their forty-five years together, I came to believe that marriage was a license to criticize rather than compliment, shame instead of show affection, and avoid instead of apologize. Not only was this relationship dynamic familiar to me, I had replicated it in my own marriage over the last few years. I also thought marriage was *supposed* to feel that way. And, as an immigrant daughter, I believed, once you're married, you're married for good. That's it. End of story.

Right...?

As I continued my drive to the city, I turned up the volume on my car speakers, I heard an answer to that question. Katherine Woodward Thomas was introducing a new concept called "conscious uncoupling," a revolutionary idea where two people bravely end a marriage with grace, generosity, and mutual respect. Honoring the relationship and the decision to commit to each other took precedence over everything else.

Thomas's trailblazing perspective spoke directly to my weary heart. I nodded my head in agreement to each relatable truth bomb she dropped. I marveled at this brilliant woman, who seemed to be describing my life exactly as it was unfolding. My mind then went to other profound words of wisdom: *my therapist's*.

In an attempt to save my struggling marriage, I had done two things: signed up for an online relationship webinar (a fairly new concept in 2011) and started marriage counseling, also a new concept, at least for me. The latter was the main reason why I was driving to Edmonton that day, to attend another therapy session with my new therapist, the next morning.

My therapist was a short, plump, immigrant from Chile. She and her husband, both psychologists, worked out of an old historic building on the south side of the city. We had met only a handful of times, but she was highly intuitive. While traditional Asians consider therapy shameful, her direct matter-of-fact approach and straight-shooting, tough-love talk actually spoke to my Asian-ness, making the long drive worth it for me.

Looking back, I also believe she could see I was in denial about my marriage, so her directness was perhaps her brave attempt to shock me with some blinding truths, so I could see more clearly and wake myself up from my slumber.

She said things in her thick Chilean accent like, "He's not married to yooooou. He's married to the toooooown!" And "Yoooou, my dearz, cannot live in that little town! For yoooou..., you are a tropical flower that needs to be repotted, so that you can bloooom!"

While her offbeat metaphors seemed amusing to me at the time, I also acknowledged that, somewhere deep down, there was truth in what she was saying. (I smile to myself as I write from my tropical home, in the Costa Rican jungle.)

After she met both Nate and me for the first time, she pulled me aside and said, "Whenz za bird and za fish fall in love, iz beautiful, but where do they live, *hmmmm*?"

She was spot on. I was the bird, and Nate was the fish. I can now see very clearly how I, an internationally influenced city girl, would fly into that little town on the lake whenever the winds changed, nest for a while, and then fly out whenever I felt the need to explore the world from a bird's-eye view again.

Nate, on the other hand, was indeed a fish in his hometown on the lake, totally in his element. The quintessential farm boy, son of a commercial fisherman (coincidence? I think not), and a proud steward of his community. He had everything he loved and needed right there, in order to be comfortable. So, whenever I mentioned wanting to move somewhere else, his discomfort surfaced. I can see how, to a fish, being forced out of his comfort zone without a solid plan seemed like a bird-brain idea and didn't feel very good to him. And, like a fish out of water, he was left gasping for oxygen.

Over my fifteen years there, I did my best to contribute to and invest in that relationship, that town, and that community, in the only ways I knew how. But in the end, the truth was I simply didn't belong there. And, in our hearts, Nate and I both knew it. We were two very different people with very different upbringings and very different dreams, living under the same roof, sleeping in the same bed, and searching for some kind of sameness in our differences. In the end, I was just an exhausted, lonely little bird doing her best to feather her nest with her self-imposed clipped wings, attempting to live like a fish…

The sun was beginning to set. As evening turned to dusk, I rolled up to the first intersection with traffic lights. I had officially entered the city limits. I butted the front of my midsize SUV to the end of a long line of pickup trucks and semi-trucks, and I let out a sigh of relief for making it to the city before dark. Squinting at the bright lights of oncoming traffic, the loud, monotonous clicking of my left-hand turn signal woke me from my bird-fish relationship analysis. I turned off the webinar and quickly shifted my focus to navigating the road in silence.

As the traffic light turned green, I diligently scoured the street signs to find my colleague's townhouse. Along with my therapist appointment in the morning, I also planned to meet up with my graphic-designer and go over some business stuff that evening, so I could make the most out of my trip.

After navigating several twists and turns through a funky residential suburb, I slid into an empty spot on a nearby bustling side street. I noticed I had made pretty good time. Maybe due to the unseasonably dry winter road conditions. Or maybe because of the overwhelming relationship reflections still swirling in my head. Whatever the reason, I was thrilled to, once again, complete another trip on Death Road and arrive safely.

After my colleague and I finalized my new business logo, I was ready for a good night's sleep. As I was packing up my things to leave, she interrupted my plan to hit the pillow early, saying, "Hey. An old friend of mine is in town, and I'm meeting up with her at her motel for a drink and a catch-up sesh. I talk about you all the time to her, and I'm sure she'd like to meet you. Why don't you come with?"

Over the last few years, I'd grown pretty good at keeping myself busy and filling even the smallest voids of loneliness or emptiness with random wine drinking, in random places, with random people. So, even though I was tired, I ignored my body and instantly replied, "Sure. That sounds fun."

A few hours later, I found myself, my colleague, and her friend in a shabby motel not unlike something out of the movie *Thelma and Louise*. All three of us were perched atop a single bed that smelled of stale cigarettes, in a room with a view of the freeway and the neon vacancy sign outside. The old, beat-up bar fridge had seen better days, and it randomly screamed out in high-pitched yelps that made us jump in fright, before we melted into a puddle of giggles each time. One bottle of cheap wine and an hour of girl talk later, the three of us were laughing and sharing stories as if we were old friends.

The two girls were recounting their horror-story dating fiascos when my colleague's friend made reference to me.

"Gosh, girl, you're so lucky. You can just have sex whenever you want!" She threw her head back, mouth wide open, and laughed out loud.

Without batting an eyelash, I blurted, "Meh, it doesn't really happen that often."

Suddenly, everything stopped. The room fell silent. All you could hear was the sickly squeal of the bar fridge and the flickering buzz of the vacancy sign outside.

She stared straight at me, her jaw slightly open, and then, very slowly, she raised her right index finger, pointed it at my head, and traced it slowly down my body in the form of an S. As she snaked slow figure eights with her finger from my head to my toes and back again, taking inventory of every curve, a guttural primal growl rolled out from the back of her throat.

"*Giiiiiiirrrrrl....!*" she roared. "Don't waste the pretty!"

I just sat there, stunned, my eyes fixed on this beautiful stranger who had known me for only an hour, yet who knew everything she needed to know.

At that moment, something inside me clicked. She was right. My Chilean therapist was right. Katherine Woodward Thomas was right. They were all right. How many times, and in how many different ways, did I have to hear what I already knew deep down? And from complete strangers, no less?

When was I finally going to admit I had spent years—over a decade—rationalizing my life and my marriage to death? I had spent a lifetime making excuses, avoiding certain truths, and completely ignoring my own intuition, my internal compass, and my fundamental needs. I was trapped by my own cultural conditioning. I had overlaid my family's Eastern traditions onto my modern Western life. No PDA. No indulgences. No apologies. No failing. Do not fail at school. Do not fail at your career. And, under any circumstance, do not fail at your marriage!

In my immigrant household growing up, the idea of failure went beyond academic or professional setbacks. It meant dishonoring cultural family values and the sacrifices of those who came before me. While some of those cultural values weren't even mine, I was trained to inhabit them, like the "good girl" and "good wife" roles that didn't necessarily reflect my own personal values, feelings, needs, or expression. They were simply roles I was expected to play, whether they fit or not.

My eyes welled up. I had avoided the discomfort, the conflict, the difficult conversations, and the deep knowing for far too long. Nate and I had grown so far apart, we could no longer see each other for who we really were: a bird and a fish.

My therapist's words haunted me. I was the bird, but would I ever truly fly? Could I break free from the weight of my heritage, the binds of loyalty to my family's expectations, and the cultural patterns that had long defined my worth? Or would I remain tethered, flapping furiously on the edge of the lake in that little northern town?

Tears bubbled up under my eyelids and threatened to spill over. Just then, the fridge squealed, breaking the silence. With that, I swiftly jumped off the bed, grabbed my bag, mumbled something about being tired, and thanked the girls for a fun evening.

I practically ran out of the motel room, barely feeling the chilly night air as hot tears streamed down my cheeks. I swung my car door open, threw my bag in the passenger seat, plunked myself down onto the hard leather seat, planted my forehead on the top of the steering wheel, and closed my eyes. After a few minutes, I started to feel cold, but I didn't move, feeling trapped behind the icy prison bars of my tear-streaked face. After sucking in a mouthful of frozen air, I exhaled a condensation-filled sigh and opened my eyes.

My bag I'd tossed on the passenger seat gaped open, as though it were yelling at me: *"What do you think everyone has been trying to tell you this entire time?"* I thrust my hand inside it and rummaged around for the car keys.

After jamming them into the ignition and cranking them around, I shivered, praying the engine would turn over on the first try. With a slight hesitation, the engine let out a loud whir *"Vrrrroooommm,"* as if to say, amid a fake cough, *"Ackh!* It sure took you long enough to figure it out, didn't it?"

Jarred out of my pity party by the thought of my bag and my car berating me for being so blind, I sat straight up, dragged my palms over my face, and took a deep breath. At that moment, I got it. I could no longer ignore the outside voices or the voice inside me—the one that had always known I wanted something different. It wasn't about abandoning Nate; it was about freeing myself—giving myself permission to live out loud, in the fullest expression of my true values, and becoming whom I was meant to be, not whoever my upbringing or tradition expected and wished me to be.

I looked at the sad woman in the rearview mirror. This was it. It was "go time." The ultimate road trip. But first, in order for me to get where I wanted to be, I needed to change directions and blindly trust the unfamiliar road that lay ahead.

I knew in my heart that this journey was going to take everything I had in me. What I didn't know was how bumpy the ride would be, how many stop signs I would hit, and how many detours I'd have to take along the way—a formidable and arduous journey not unlike driving down Death Road after dark during a northern Canadian winter.

I reached for the seatbelt, slung it across my shoulder, buckled myself in, and gripped the steering wheel tightly. As my silent screams got louder, I prepared for the ride of my life. I could feel the Polar Express ride speeding up, and all I could do was hang on for dear life.

Chapter 2
IMMIGRIT

Dad

MY DAD WAS BORN in Peshawar, a small northern town in what then was India in 1934. He grew up in a Hindu family with his parents and ten siblings. Yes, *eleven* children. When I pause to think about that, I marvel at the sheer magnitude of my Indian grandmother's feminine strength. She spent more than twenty years of her life breastfeeding.

My grandfather was a government contractor who benefited from the ripple effects of the World War II. He was a crucial supply hub for the British forces who were stationed in Peshawar, supplying military personnel with basic staples like food, hardware, and imported goods.

My dad was twelve years old when India gained its independence from British rule in 1947. At that time, an imaginary line was drawn across the land, separating India from what is now Pakistan. It was a monumental historical shift—the largest mass migration in human history, which would forever alter the trajectory of tens of millions of lives for generations to come, including mine.

As political divisions between India and Pakistan deepened, so did volatility and military presence. My dad recalls jumping over bodies in the streets that had once been a playground for him and his siblings. What was recently a safe haven suddenly teemed with men in uniform, their rifles slung over their shoulders. The visible military presence in residential neighborhoods triggered fear and uncertainty in the hearts and minds of millions of civilians, becoming a weapon in itself. Under the guise of "protection," fear was used to forge political and religious partitioning aimed to divide and conquer. In this case, Muslims and Hindus. And Peshawar fell on the Muslim side. Since my dad's family home was now on the Pakistani side of the line, they couldn't stay there. But they certainly tried.

For an entire year, in the name of safety, my dad's family decided to follow the region's social, political, and religious norms. My dad and his siblings went to Muslim schools, learned Arabic and Urdu, changed their names to Muslim names, studied the Qur'an, hung Allah on the wall—and my grandmother wore a burqa. But as the political landscape shifted and divisions intensified, word spread that a Hindu family was still living in Peshawar.

One evening, two men came to the house. They began asking my grandfather some probing questions, testing him to see how he would react to the idea of converting his family to the Muslim faith... Most notably, whether they had already converted. My grandfather, who apparently had quite a temper, didn't take kindly to this line of questioning, and the conversation quickly escalated.

My dad's second-eldest brother was a sharp, intelligent young man in his twenties with an impressive presence of mind. He had a natural ability to think quickly on his feet, which earned him the respect of the entire family, including his parents'. My uncle was considered the primary father figure by his younger siblings, nieces, and nephews, and they deferred to him, even into their old age. He later became known to me as my "yogi uncle."

As the exchange between my grandfather, my uncle, and the men grew more heated, one of the soldiers blurted out the ultimate threat: removing the women and children from the house. As my yogi uncle attempted to redirect their attention, my twelve-year-old dad appeared from behind them and stood in front of my grandfather and uncle.

My dad was a handsome boy—dark hair, fair skin, big bright eyes, and a wide, straight-toothed smile. Struck by his good looks, one of the men turned to the other and questioned their threat. How could they take this beautiful child away from his family? After some hesitation, they backed down, convincing themselves to leave for now.

However, my shrewd yogi uncle knew better. He understood this was only a temporary reprieve, a stark warning of what was to come. He knew their time in Peshawar was quickly running out.

With the help of his Caucasian British boss, my yogi uncle devised a plan for the family to leave Peshawar, under the radar. From there, a car would take them to the airstrip, where the Indian government was helping its Hindu citizens migrate to safety in the capital city of New Delhi.

My grandfather and yogi uncle left first, pretending they were going to work. My dad and one of his brothers dressed in layers of clothing, grabbed their field hockey sticks, and dashed out the door as if headed for a game. My grandmother made it seem as though she was taking my youngest aunt and uncle to the market, her burqa concealing pots and pans underneath it.

They all made their way to the meeting point. My dad recalled his immense relief and quiet celebration each time another family member arrived safely. The plan worked. My yogi uncle managed to get all of his siblings and their parents to safety. I, for one, am forever grateful to my yogi uncle for his foresight, perspicacity, and courage—without him, I might not be here today.

After the harrowing escape, my dad and his family lived in the Old Fort refugee camp in New Delhi for a year. Eventually, through my uncle's resourcefulness, they were able to procure homes—some of which are still in our family today.

When he was fifteen years old, as a result of refugee life, my dad contracted tuberculosis and ended up in the hospital and ill for nearly two years. Once again, my yogi uncle came to the rescue. He worked three jobs to save enough money for an experimental drug that ended up saving my dad's life. Having missed two years of school, my dad had to redo his senior academic year. While this setback was hardly a sacrifice compared to being alive, the label "academic failure" stuck with him. It seemed to me he spent the rest of his life proving he—and anyone else he cared about—would never be such a failure again.

As in many Asian cultures, the highest goal in life is a good education. And, as with any goal, there is sacrifice. Parents often gave up their own education to fund their children's schooling, and, if necessary, older siblings sacrificed theirs to support the younger ones'. The cycle continued like this. So, after high school, instead of applying to college, my dad followed tradition and sought a job to support his family and help educate his younger siblings. But my yogi uncle had other plans for his studious younger brother.

Because India was a British colony at the time, India's forced participation in World War II without consultation meant my brilliant uncle was conscripted to fight, sacrificing his own college dreams for his country and his family. When he found out my dad hadn't applied to college and had missed the deadline, he was furious. There was no way he was going to let any of his younger siblings, starting with my dad, repeat his fate. He knew my dad had what it took to excel, and he refused to let him squander such a valuable opportunity. So, once again, my yogi uncle took matters into his own hands in order to get my dad into college.

Since my dad had come in at the top of his high school class at Jamia Millia Islamia College, a public school founded by Muslim leaders, and was friends with the Chancellor's son, my yogi uncle asked the Chancellor to call in a favor. Despite having missed the application deadline, my dad received a glowing recommendation from the Chancellor himself, a four-year scholarship, and admission to Delhi University. Ironically, the same religion that had forced his family out of their home in Peshawar was also the one that offered him an opportunity to fulfill his dreams. The Universe works in mysterious ways.

My dad was smart, hardworking, and had the looks of a Bollywood actor. He easily could have pursued a career in film, but his commitment to stability and success overshadowed any desire to dance and lip-sync his way through Bollywood. Besides, in university, he developed a passion for a life beyond India's borders. Back then, Indian university students harbored big dreams. Their country had been ruled by England for so long, they were acutely aware of the Western world. They dreamed of leaving India to explore, study, work, and find success abroad.

So, after graduating from Delhi University, my dad took a bold step and moved to England to live out his dream. He said goodbye to his family and prepared for the month-long boat trip to London.

At the time, the Indian government had imposed strict limitations on the amount of money one could take abroad—just enough to get you there, but not enough to let you stay. Luckily for him, my dad's younger brother wasn't much of a rule-follower and was clever enough to work around them. A talented and well sought-after professional photographer in Simla, my uncle had VIP access to most places in India without being questioned. Unorthodox and a rebel without a cause in his own way, my *rebel* uncle possessed a vision and scope far beyond his camera lens. So, armed with his camera and his charm, he got onto the boat without a hitch.

Just before they parted ways, my rebel uncle hugged my dad goodbye. Later, my dad discovered a hidden stash of money in his front jacket pocket. This was it. His mission was clear: not just for himself, but for his entire family, especially his younger brother and siblings. At that moment, my dad didn't know it, but he was already carving a path for himself—and for them—to build new lives in England and, eventually, Canada.

Whether it was the tuberculosis scare, his college experience, or the unwavering faith his brothers had in him, my dad was driven by a deep hunger for something more—something he couldn't yet understand. His dedication, risk-taking, and hard work got him where he is today. These are the reasons I was born in a first-world country and able to write this book in my native English tongue.

When my dad first arrived in England, he stayed with an Indian friend who had been in London for several months. Together, they paid room and board to an older Jamaican woman whose food, my dad says (while curling his nose), "I ate to survive." My dad lost weight, not only from eating less, but also from walking the streets every day in the rain in search of work, resulting in a painful case of kidney stones. Yet, my gritty dad didn't let it slow him down and kept pounding pavement. As a skilled accountant, he eventually found a job and quickly worked his way up. From making pennies an hour to earning more than his friend, my dad managed to afford his own place to live in less than three months.

Scouring the newspaper ads, he found a room for rent and called the number listed. A woman with a high-pitched voice answered, "Yessss, it's available. Why don't you come by and see it?"

Unfamiliar with the location, my dad used the little money he had left to take the bus only a few blocks away. Disappointed that he could have easily walked and saved a few bucks, he went up to the front door and knocked. It was barely a tap before the door swung open. A tall, middle-aged, gray-haired Caucasian woman with worry lines on her forehead stood in the doorway.

She took one look at my dad's brown face, scowled, and in the same high-pitched voice, yelled, "It's gone!" As she slammed the door, she muttered something about, "Your kind."

But my dad wasn't one to back down. He walked to the nearest payphone, inserted one of his last coins, and dialed the number on the crumpled newspaper ad.

The same high-pitched voice answered, "Hellooo?" In the same kind tone that he had heard on the phone earlier, she said, "Yesssss, it's available. Why don't you come by and see it?"

My dad thanked her and hung up the phone.

That moment when the door slammed in his face marked a turning point in his life. It was then that he vowed to work hard enough to buy his own home. Not just for himself, but so he could offer a place to anyone who needed it—regardless of the color of their skin.

And that's exactly what he did. Over and over again.

***

Mom

My mom was born in Penang, Malaysia, in 1939, the year World War II broke out. Her childhood was shaped by rationed meals, an undercurrent of fear, and a scarcity mindset. This was all she knew. And her parents were no strangers to hardship, either.

My Chinese grandmother, a resilient woman from Canton, China, ran away from home as a young girl and escaped the fate of foot-binding, a traditional Chinese practice where young girls' feet were tightly bound to alter their size; tiny feet were considered a symbol of beauty and status. Needless to say, my Chinese grandmother lacked maternal nurturing and ended up finding respite and solace in my grandfather. They emigrated to Malaysia, eventually moving to Singapore, where my grandfather managed a rubber tree plantation, and together, they raised six kids.

I didn't know my Chinese grandmother well, and our communication was limited by the language barrier (I didn't speak Cantonese, and she didn't speak English). However, there is one thing I'm certain of: I come from a long line of fierce women. All fighters in their own right, my mom (now weighing barely seventy-five pounds and wearing a size four shoe) has challenged everything and everyone, including life itself, for as long as I can remember. From war to warrior, my mother is probably the tiniest but toughest cookie you'll ever meet. Part of her armor is the fierce sense of autonomy and self-sufficiency she developed as a consequence of her lineage, including the war experiences. She also carries a deep-seated fear and memory of survival.

My mom, the third eldest of six children, remembers sensing that her own mother favored some of her other siblings, leaving her feeling insignificant and unloved. This feeling of being overlooked stemmed not just from intuition, but also from the most primal of wartime experiences: food.

Rationed meals created a strict pecking order. My grandfather got to choose the choicest cuts of meat first, followed by the eldest and youngest kids. The remaining family members, which included my mother, got to eat whatever was left. Still to this day, when presented with a plate of food, my mother asks if everyone else has already eaten.

Other seemingly small yet profoundly impactful moments were etched into my mom's memory, like the way life shifted once the war ended. My mom remembers how she and her school-aged siblings were made to stay home to manage themselves and study, while her mother took the younger children to the market or to the cinema—luxuries that had been off-limits during the war.

As a young girl, my mom didn't feel particularly close to her mother, and as a result, she learned to find comfort in solitude, developing an early sense of independence. As a young adult, she immersed herself in reading, learning, and dreaming of traveling alone. Subconsciously, she made the decision never to rely on anyone for anything—especially not for attention or love. This invincible independence became the driving force behind this hard-shelled, (then) one-hundred-pound force of nature who traveled across three continents before she turned thirty.

My Chinese grandfather was a trusting man with a big heart and an even bigger dream. Despite the political and social unrest in Singapore, both pre- and post-war, he worked tirelessly to build a life for his family. As Britain and Japan battled for control of the island, my grandfather's belief remained unwavering: if he could give his children a good education, they could leave Singapore and live peacefully anywhere in the world. He was right.

When his daughters were ready for college, my grandfather knew that two of the most reliable—and "suitable"—careers for women in the fifties were nursing and teaching. So, he sent all of his daughters to college abroad. My mom ended up studying to be a teacher at the University of London in England.

An innately curious, book-smart, yet naïve seventeen-year-old, my mom thrived while living and studying abroad. She came alive whenever she had the chance to travel, immerse herself in new cultures, and experience life beyond the sheltered confines of her upbringing. She journeyed from England to France, where she worked as a nanny, learned French, and taught English to her host family.

In 1965, my mom and her younger sister, who was also living in London, decided to join an international student trip to Wales. Coincidentally, my dad and his friend went on the same trip. When the four of them met on that fateful journey, my mom and dad fell in love. And, yes, you guessed it—my aunt and now uncle did, too. Although no boat was involved, I still refer to this pivotal event as *The Love Boat*, a lighthearted romantic comedy series set aboard a cruise ship during the late 1970s.

But, like most love stories, *The Love Boat* soon capsized. The fantasy of living as an interracial couple in 1960s London quickly lost its glamour for my newlywed parents when the political climate shifted dramatically. In 1968, Enoch Powell's infamous "River of Blood" speech was given. It targeted South Asians, particularly Indians, resulting is widespread discrimination and hostility. Despite being professional, hardworking, and legal permanent residents of England, my parents encountered fierce racial backlash, including verbal and physical aggression, and were treated as second-class citizens.

So, when a Canadian superintendent of schools visited London in search of new teachers, my mom saw an opportunity and applied. She was offered a teaching position in Alberta, Canada. Knowing little about Canada and virtually nothing about Alberta, she accepted, and this marked the beginning of an entirely new chapter for my parents. They would once again leave their family and friends behind, this time for a remote, northern country known for its frozen tundra and Wild West persona.

My dad recalls going to the library to look up *Edmonton, Alberta* in an encyclopedia. There, he found a brief description featuring words like "prairies," "vast landscapes," and "cold winters." With that knowledge and the experience of their current social climate, they sold their home in London, packed their bags, and embarked on a journey to a place far removed from anything they had known before.

In 1968, my mom flew to Canada first, eager to start her job in the fall, while my dad undertook the onerous task of hauling trunkloads of their precious belongings to Canada. He took a week-long boat ride from London to Montreal, then from there, he travelled across the large country by train to Edmonton, Alberta, in the dead of winter.

For those who are familiar with Edmonton's winter of 1969, you'll know that T-shirts were made afterward that read, *I survived the cold-snap of 1969*. For twenty-six days straight, temperatures ranged from 6°F to a bone-chilling minus-40°F.

My Asian parents were painfully unprepared for this kind of cold. They didn't have winter coats, boots, or a car. They often tell the story of their first week in Edmonton, walking through knee-deep snow drifts to buy groceries, clad in nothing but light jackets, no hats or gloves, and low-top leather-soled shoes. They were cold. But they were cold together. And that's what being an immigrant is all about: sacrifice, survival, and venturing into the unknown.

Why such a sacrifice? Because an immigrant's singular focus is to build a better life than the one they left behind. Immigrants know that hard work is the ticket to achieving their dreams. They also understand that the fruits of their labor can be fleeting or snatched away at any moment—often for reasons beyond their control. It's a constant dance of living with both fear and gratitude, side by side.

My parents were among the lucky ones. They spoke fluent English, had good educations, and had job experience in a Western country. But others might argue that luck had little to do with it. They made it to North America because of their relentless drive, hard work, and tenacious grit.

Yes, immigrants have grit. It's an essential quality for survival and success. They can't afford to be afraid of hard work, risk-taking, or starting over if necessary. The lives they create for themselves—and their families—depend on the strength of that grit.

I call it *immigrit*.

And I inherited *immigrit*. It's in my blood.

***

Me

Immigrit has gifted me with a powerful resilience that enables me to dive into anything whole-heartedly, then to fall down and get back up, only to do it all over again. I'm not a quitter. I don't give up easily, and I like to win. In fact, I have quite successfully started, stopped, and restarted almost every facet of my life: jobs, careers, businesses, fields of study, homes, cities, countries, and relationships... The list goes on. Coupled with my maternal lineage of female fierceness, immigrit has taken me far in life. Yet it has also held me back, stood in my way, and drop-kicked me in more ways than I'd like to admit.

As much as immigrit has helped me create success in my life, it has also fostered a deeply ingrained feeling of guilt within me. For my parents, and most first-generation immigrants, success meant sacrificing everything for a good education, so you could get a good job, make good money, and put a good roof over your head and good food on your table. Rinse and repeat. However, this was considered just the baseline for success. *Real success* to an immigrant parent is when *their kids become more successful than they are.*

Yep, we children of immigrants are the whole reason why our parents did what they did. They took a risk for *us*. They sacrificed their own opportunities for *ours*. They sacrificed their own families for *ours*. They sacrificed their own joy and wins for *ours*. Some even sacrificed their own lives for *ours*.

As a result, there is an underlying understanding between second-generation immigrant kids and our first-generation immigrant parents. Unbeknownst to us, before most of us were even born, we somehow struck a deal with our parents that we would pay them back through our success. This deal came with one critical caveat. Should we ever manage to disappoint our parents, we had better be prepared to experience the deep, nagging, guilt that breathes fire down our necks, like a dragon threatening to leave permanent scars, forever reminding us of this ultimate betrayal.

I call it *immiguilt*.

Immiguilt is the unspoken understanding between immigrant parents and their kids, an ugly unspoken mess of expectations, perceptions, cultural biases, obligation, shame, loyalties, resentment, and guilt. The very nature of this confusing cultural and relational dynamic sets us all up for the highest chance for failure.

And fail, I did. Over and over and over again. Whether it is signaled by a click of the tongue, a disapproving look, the silent treatment, or worse, every child of immigrants knows the exact moment when they've disappointed their parents. Immiguilt washes over them like a tidal wave. For me, let's just say disappointment became my middle name, and immiguilt was the game.

I ended up inadvertently breaking my end of the bargain often. Just by being me. My perceived lack of interest is my character flaw. My perceived lack of motivation is a personal attack on their parenting. My perceived failure is their failure. My dreams are to remain just that, dreams. And if I so much as dared to follow them, immiguilt would be right there with me, ready to jolt me back into reality.

That said, immiguilt is also a choice. While every kid of immigrant parents is a product of their immigrit environment, we also get to decide how much immiguilt we will allow ourselves to carry. Immigrit and immiguilt breed and fuel each other in a self-deprecating cultural-conditioning loop that pulls you away from making decisions aligned to you and your heart.

In my case, feeling indebted to my parents caused me to consistently put pressure on myself to follow the rules, to be "successful," and to *win* at all costs, in the hope that, someday, I would *make them proud*. Immiguilt thrust me into a vicious cycle of proving I can "win" something (or someone), only to feel deeply dissatisfied once I got it.

While this relentless drive to win has gotten me a lot in life, it has also regrettably cost me much more. While I've created extraordinary opportunities and striking successes for myself through immigrit, immiguilt is responsible for my many colossal failures and missed opportunities. Immigrit and immiguilt have driven most of my decisions in my life, fueled my drive to succeed, and plunged me into a woeful aftermath of losing everything, especially myself.

Immigrit was also the key that opened many doors for my dad. As an accountant for a few companies in England and Canada, my dad took his job very seriously. When nobody else dared, my dad showed up to work in the thickest of London's fog, worked long hours to finish projects in record time, and caught errors that his superiors missed. His potential was notable, and he managed to climb company ranks in short order—immigrit.

One such example was when the "big boss" (whom most people in my dad's position would never even have had the chance to meet) asked my dad to take a short plane ride with him from Edmonton to Calgary. This was the first time my dad ever set foot on a plane. He didn't know why he was on it or where he was going. He just went.

After landing in what could only be described as the Wild West, my dad's boss asked him if he had enjoyed the plane ride. My dad answered sheepishly, "Yes, very much."

"Well, good then," his boss replied. "Because we're expanding our business, and this will be your new home."

This promotion to become the boss's right-hand-man in greener pastures (literally and figuratively) permitted my dad to realize his promise to himself, to buy his own home. My dad traveled back and forth from Calgary to Edmonton until my mom managed to get a teaching job with the Calgary Board of Education.

This ended up being the last chapter on my parents' long journey across the globe. They settled in Calgary and worked hard to build a life for themselves and, eventually, for their children. My sister was born in Calgary in the early seventies, and then I was, two years later. My dad's dream of raising a family in a home he owned was now a reality.

My parents chose to live in suburbia, where the houses were big, the yards were bigger, and the people were, well, White. Situated thirty minutes from the central downtown core, our neighborhood consisted of mostly older, White, upper-middle-class, retired married couples. Not only were we the only non-White family in the entire neighborhood, we were the only house for miles with young kids. This made for some pretty lonely bike rides around the neighborhood. The most exciting incidents for a nine-year-old were scarfing down handfuls of ripe raspberries before getting caught, managing to squeeze nectar out of those tiny white Twinberry flowers, or "getting air" on the small jump at the bottom of the Willacy hill.

Growing up, I spent a lot of time alone, in my head. As a result, I developed a brilliant imagination. I could conjure up thrilling adventures, triggered by some of the most mundane real-life events. I often found myself sitting on the patio in the backyard, watching ants scurry around for hours. I'd imagine their underground playground, them marching through tunnels and filling up tiny wheelbarrows with dirt, while exchanging quick hellos and high-fives to one another in passing. Or I'd climb up the pussywillow tree and lean off to one side, aboard an imaginary pirate ship, lost at sea and in search of treasure.

One summer, the tallest tree in our yard fell down in a thunderstorm and landed smack-dab in the middle of our backyard. The hours of joy felt endless as I explored the dark, mysterious caves on this "deserted island," which had magically appeared before my very eyes. How disappointing it was when the rumblings of a chainsaw interrupted my fantasy, and my dad cut up my island into pieces of firewood. Those adventures in our backyard are some of my fondest childhood memories.

The most real-life action I remember in our cul-de-sac was when, one evening, dinner was interrupted by red and white lights strobing through the picture windows of our front room. Curious yet cautious, I ran to the front window, peeled back the curtains, and peered out onto the front street. An ambulance was parked in front of our neighbors' house. We found out later that poor Mr. Alcorn had just had his second heart attack.

Another real-life event that interested the inquisitive, nine-year-old me was when our other neighbor's adult kids came over to visit them. I remember thinking how cool the "Dunmire girls" were: in their twenties, with short, feathered haircuts, bellbottom cords, and hooped earrings. Whenever I saw their car parked outside of their parents' house, I'd wait at the bottom of our driveway for a glimpse. To pass the time, I'd find some random things to do in our pristine front yard, like move the decorative rocks from one side of the bush to the other, gather bunches of pussy willows, or pluck the heads off dandelions, unwittingly spreading the seeds across the lawn. (My dad was certainly not thrilled about this last pastime.)

When the Dunmire girls finally left, I'd stare at them longingly with a wide grin across my face and my puppy-dog eyes. "Notice me, notice me, notice me...," I whispered under my breath.

Most times, they'd look over, flash me a toothy smile, and send me a friendly wave before getting into their car and driving off. Sometimes, though, they'd come over and talk to me. *Yes!* They smiled sweetly as they sauntered over to where I was pretending to be hard at work in the yard. I don't really remember our conversations, but I do remember how kind they were to me and how they hugged me goodbye.

Yes, I always looked forward to those hugs. Despite my seriously self-reliant, individualistic side, I was also a clingy kid who craved touch. When I was four, my parents took me to India for the first time, and I clung onto my older cousins so much, they nicknamed me *chipkali*, meaning gecko in Hindi. Geckos have sticky fingers and are hard to pry off. While I still marvel sometimes at the creative, independent, free-spirited side of me, I also realize how much connection, attention, and touch I craved, seeking it out wherever and whenever I could. This carried over well into adulthood.

My parents were not huggers and considered showing affection to be excessive and unnecessary. I don't remember being coddled when we were sad or our boo-boos kissed when we were hurt. I never expected to be hugged hello, goodbye, or goodnight. There were no "I love yous" or "I'm proud of yous" or "Good jobs."

Holidays were "just another day," because consumerism was a made-up concept in the West and a "waste of money." We had what we needed, and life was *good*. We lived in a good house in a good neighborhood, ate a lot of good food (to be fair, our kitchen cupboard did look like the cookie aisle in Safeway), went to a good school, and participated in plenty of good extracurricular activities. Ah, the extracurricular activities.

Asian extracurricular activities are not the same as Western ones. Western extracurricular activities are typically sports, introduced in school and then carried over as "extra" activities in the evening because kids actually enjoy or even develop a passion for the activity. Further, those kids are usually pretty good at them.

Asian extracurricular activities, however, are not actually "extra" at all. They're essential. Every weeknight and weekend are jam-packed with many activities you are not actually required to like, enjoy, or be good at. In fact, one would argue it was preferable that you weren't good at these activities at first, so your immigrant parents had something to brag about to other immigrant parents once you had rapidly excelled in said activity.

And so, between my sister and me, we endured hours upon hours of mandatory lessons in tap dance, ballet, piano, violin, orchestra, music theory, band, swimming, gymnastics, skating, ringette, horseback riding, creative writing, theater, public speaking, martial arts, bike repair, and… Chinese school. Ah yes, Chinese school.

First of all, Chinese school was on Saturdays—not ideal for young Western-born kids, who'd spent their entire week hunched over desks and whose friends' weekends were reserved for camping, skiing, birthday parties, and fun. Second, my sister and I were the only kids who were half Chinese instead of full Chinese. We did not speak Cantonese or ever hear it spoken at home; therefore, due to our shortcomings, and in perfectly *extra* extracurricular form, my sister and I were made to stay inside during every break for *"extra* study."

While we listened to all the other kids laughing and playing outside, we wrote out Chinese characters repeatedly: mountain, mountain, mountain... Water, water, water... Or made to figure out the storyline for cartoons with dozens of incomprehensible speech balloons. Moreover, they changed our names to Cantonese names: Cao Lok and Cai An.

Whenever the teacher spoke in her quick, high-pitched Cantonese, she ended the sentence abruptly and turned toward us. Once my sister and I realized that she was talking to one of us, we'd hiss at each other back and forth. "That's you!" "No! It's you!"

After countless complaints to our mom, Chinese school didn't last long, but the Asian-influenced Saturdays continued. Chinese school was merely replaced with orchestra practice and gymnastics in the morning, and music and theory lessons in the afternoon.

Life in our home was simple and direct. Everybody knew their role, what their job was (a.k.a. school), and stayed in their lane. We all got along (for the most part). Love was implied, and nobody felt more special or more important than anybody else. Immigrit.

Yet, outside our home was a different story and far from simple. One time, as my sister and I were playing in the backyard, our neighbor was also outside in her yard. As usual, we were giggling and carrying on like the young, innocent girls we were, when suddenly the doorbell rang. Yay! Company!

My sister and I rushed excitedly through the house to see who it was. When we got close, we could see our mom speaking with a visibly concerned white-haired woman at the front door. Our excitement quickly subsided when we realized it was just old Mrs. Alcorn.

But something was off. She seemed bothered, speaking to our mom in a shrill tone. I wondered, did Mr. Alcorn have another heart attack?

Catching a glimpse of us cowering behind the wall, she waved her hands in our direction and then pointed one gnarled, white finger with a red-painted tip at us. "Your kids...," she stammered.

Uh-oh. She's talking about us. Were we in trouble? Had we disturbed the peace and quiet of her retirement with our innocent squeals of childhood joy and laughter in the backyard?

"Your kids...," she spat out again.

Shoot. We were definitely in trouble.

"Your kids...," she repeated a third time. "They speak just like us... Canadians!"

Silence.

We all just stood there, staring at Mrs. Alcorn. *Wait a second.* I was confused. Was she upset that we were speaking like them? Was she asking my mom if we were Canadian? Or was she trying to tell my mom that we weren't? And what did "speak just like us Canadians" even mean, I wondered.

My mom finally broke the silence. "*Umm*, yes, Mrs. Alcorn," she said slowly. "That's because they're Canadian."

Not getting the answer she was looking for, and looking just as confused as I was feeling, Mrs. Alcorn tightened her red lips, curled up her nose, then turned around and left in a huff. My mom closed the door behind her and went back to whatever she was doing in the kitchen without saying a word.

Baffled by what had just occurred and our mom's not explaining it, I went back outside to sit in the silence of the culture gap. I didn't get it. We didn't get in trouble, so why then did people seem so bothered by us?

When I was younger, racial microaggressions left me feeling confused, helpless, and even guilty at times—immiguilt. And while I didn't always understand what was happening, I just knew it felt wrong.

One day, my mom and I stopped at the grocery store on our way home to quickly grab a few things for dinner. We were standing in one of the regular check-out lines with a basket full of items when the twelve-items-or-less express aisle came available. The young girl at the express register looked at us, glanced at our basket, nodded, and motioned for us to approach her till.

When we got there, my mom said, "Oh, but we have fourteen items."

"No problem. Close enough!" the girl chimed with a smile.

As she proceeded to check us out, swiping our items swiftly through the till, a tall, White man came up behind us and stood in line. He laughed out loud for everyone to hear and then, in a loud and sarcastic tone, said, "Ha! Well, clearly *some* people can't read English." Then, he pointed his chin toward the twelve-or-less sign and after, to my mom.

I looked up at her. She just stood there, silent and staring straight ahead. The cashier, clearly uncomfortable, quickly handed my mom the receipt, and we left.

On the way to the car, my mother's fuming silence broke. "How *dare* he! That fool! I could probably teach *him* English!"

To have to watch racial microaggressions or, worse, overt racism play out against your own parents is a deeply painful and confusing experience for a child of immigrants. It was like half of me was being insulted and the other half was doing the insulting. And there was absolutely nothing I or any of us could do about it.

Even when I was an adult, my Canadian accent, coupled with my brown face and Asian eyes, sparked a confusion most people couldn't hide. Or hide well, at least. And this showed me people's true colors.

I remember calling a store to ask if they carried a specific item, hoping a phone call could save me an hour drive there and back plus some gas. The lady on the other end was jovial and friendly, and even went the extra mile to ask me to "kindly hold," while she went to look for the item.

When she found the last one in the store, she celebrated with me on the phone, put it aside for me, and then said enthusiastically, "Just come on over to the customer service desk. Ask for Linda, and I'll have it waiting here for you!"

When I got to the store, I walked over to the customer service desk and said to one of the three women behind it, "Hi, I'm looking for Linda. I called earlier, and she was kind enough to put something aside for me."

A middle-aged white woman facing away from me in the far back corner exclaimed joyfully, "I'm Linda!" and then swiftly turned around with a smile. When she saw me, though, the only customer at the desk, her face went blank, her smile turned flat, and she even dropped the pen she was holding in her hand. Without a word, she awkwardly rummaged around underneath the counter, grabbed a box, rang it through, and without so much as looking up at me, tossed the receipt on the counter before walking away. Like my dad's experience in London, this Linda was nothing like the Linda I had spoken to on the phone earlier.

It's a strange feeling, knowing that someone is treating you or someone you love in a particular way because of the color of your skin or the shape of your eyes. I am also grateful to say that these incidents were the exception to the rule and not the norm in my beloved hometown. Now, fifty years later, it has become a multicultural magnet and one of Canada's vibrant international hubs.

Still, I always wondered why we never talked about it as a family, though. We didn't speak about my parents' interracial marriage, what it was like living as biracial children, or what race and racism even was. If I myself had experienced subtle and not-so-subtle racism, I could only imagine how many stories and experiences my parents had that went untold.

After all, they aren't called the "Silent Generation" for nothing.

Maybe it's because nobody really had an answer. Maybe it's because my parents didn't know what to say. Or maybe they believed that not talking about it might make it stop or go away. Perhaps they were just tired of talking about it. They had grown up during a World War, lived in "White countries" since their early twenties and knew that getting upset about racial biases was futile. So, they just focused on what they could control: work, education, paying their bills, and creating a good, honest living for themselves and their family.

I also think my parents felt somewhat helpless when it came to us kids. As much as they would have liked to, they knew they couldn't protect us from getting hurt, they couldn't understand what it was like to grow up in a Western world, and we couldn't understand the world they had left behind.

We had grown up in completely different worlds, during completely different eras, and with completely different cultural norms. Furthermore, none of us possessed the communication skills or the desire to process our feelings. Thus, there was an unspoken rule of silence. Immigrit toughens you up and requires that you "get over" your feelings fast. Traditionally, Asians consider emotions as signs of weakness, instability, immaturity, and even disrespect. Ah, tradition.

Something happens to tradition, though, when two immigrants cross over a border and have their children on the other side of it. Not only does tradition mean something completely different to their kids than it does to them. If left unspoken long enough, tradition inevitably gets lost in translation. And what's left in the silence is a culture gap.

This gap almost always breaks the unspoken traditional threads of understanding between immigrant parents and their kids. This unavoidable chasm between cultures is often a place of deep hurt, silent misunderstandings, and assumptions based on one's own version of tradition. And it's in this gap where tradition will either die hard and fast or a slow, stubborn death. Either way, the fundamental meaning of tradition dies, and a part of each of us, on either side of the gap, dies along with it.

The gap became a chasm for me, because, in addition to a culture gap, my dad was forty and my mom was thirty-six when I was born, so there was a significant generational gap between us, as well. And so, my work has been to build bridges. First, from me to myself, and then, from me to my parents.

Since the gap was so wide, it was going to take enormous effort, empathy, and understanding on my part to build a bridge across this gap. And because my immigrant parents were too busy putting food on the table and a roof over our heads, they didn't have the time, skill, or awareness to put in the work.

So, it was up to me to begin the rebuilding process by myself. I do this by remembering that, no matter what was said or done (or not said or not done) in the gap, I always knew they had my best interests at heart and loved me deeply. This unconditional love and dutiful sacrifice for the other is the unspoken rule throughout my family's history. It's the undying thread that has kept our family intact, transcending generations, borders, and cultures.

Keeping with the tradition of sacrifice—my parents' family members sacrificing for them, my parents sacrificing for us—it's now my turn, me sacrificing for them. I call it daughter-duty. And while this cultural understanding of sacrifice due to unconditional love within blood bonds is a "done thing," I'm also ready to sacrifice something different. I'm ready to sacrifice my loyalty to immigrit, immiguilt, and patterns of familial conditioning.

Daughter-duty means mustering up as much humility, curiosity, and forgiveness as I can. It means speaking up and giving voice to myself and millions of immigrant daughters so that, together, we can break the silence that lives within the gap.

It means learning to communicate with our immigrant parents in a way that repairs and rebuilds the broken parts of the bridge that dangles between us. And it means it's possible that, one day, we can all stand proudly on a solid bridge, knowing that nothing was left unsaid.

Chapter 3
BUSTER BROWN

IN 1978, I WAS A bright, effervescent four-year-old with brown skin, slanted eyes, silver-capped teeth, and a big, round, black bowl cut. Yes, literally a bowl cut. Allow me to explain.

My mom had decided that managing two kids virtually alone, plus a home while holding a full-time teaching career was too much for her. And, since my dad was doing well financially, she decided to quit her teaching job and stay at home to take care of my sister and me full time. She was in charge of the house and home and everything and everyone in it. And she did a damn good job. My mom was our chef, chauffeur, tutor, housekeeper, seamstress, nurse, taskmaster, disciplinarian—and our hairdresser.

She decided to take a hairdressing course in her "spare time." Which brings me back to the bowl cut. Let's just say my sister and I were the lucky recipients of her newfound talent (and a newly acquired set of bowls!).

One weekend that summer, my dad and I were getting ready to go out. I was excited. My dad is an extremely kind and loving man with a huge heart and a short fuse. He loves his family fiercely; working hard to provide was his way of showing that love. When I was growing up, he was the more affectionate, emotional, and vulnerable of my two parents. Dad was the voice of reason whenever Mom wouldn't budge on something. He was the safe haven when Mom threatened to discipline us with the fly swatter, and he was the softer place to land whenever we needed it.

Unlike my mom, my dad wasn't afraid to show his own emotions. He would joke with us often, carry us when we were tired, and let his tears flow when he couldn't hold them in any longer. (To this day, I have yet to see my mom cry.) I even remember, when I was three, complaining that my dad's well-groomed mustache prickled my face when he kissed me, and so... he shaved it off! When my dad *did* get mad, upset, or yell at us, however, we knew it was for something significant.

I had just gotten a brand-new pair of Buster Brown shoes, a classic set of chestnut-brown leather Mary Janes with a buckle-up T-strap and rounded toe box. Exquisite!

I sat on the second step of the stairs that led down to the basement. Those basement stairs doubled as our family shoe rack. On the short end of each red shag-carpeted step sat at least one shoebox. And nestled lovingly inside each box sat one pair of barely scuffed shoes, sandwiched between thin blankets of its original tissue paper. Both my parents have a particular appreciation for shoes, which is something I inherited.

Spinning the brand-new Buster Brown shoebox slowly in my hands as if on a rotating cake stand, I ran my fingers along the side of the box and, like reading braille, traced the lines of the Buster Brown mascot—a kid and his dog. The nondescript boy had shoulder-length blond hair and wore a red beret with a big, blue bow around his neck. With one big, blue eye open and the other closed, he winked at me as though he knew something I didn't. His secret seemed shared with the toothy, grinning dog by his side. I tipped the box to examine the lid and started to read the letters scrawled on top, my inquisitive eyes studying every letter.

As I've mentioned, I was a curious little girl who was fascinated by the world around her. I naturally spent my days observing, imagining, learning, thinking, talking, drawing, and expressing myself through art, craft, words, and movement. I was also in a French immersion preschool at the time, where I had learned to sound out each syllable in order to make out any unrecognizable words.

I stared at the letters on the shoebox and, one by one, sounded out each letter, then each syllable. Then, I strung them together like my teacher had taught us. I began to pronounce each letter out loud

Bu...

Busssss...

Bussssttttt

Busssstttte

Bussstttterrrrr

My dad's loving voice broke my train of thought behind me. "Okay, beta," (a Hindi term of endearment, like "darling," used to address one's child), he said in his usual sing-songy voice and thick Indian accent. "It's time to go!"

He walked behind me down the narrow corridor leading to the garage at the top of the basement stairs, where even more shoes were stacked.

I opened my shoebox, peeled back the tissue paper, pulled out one of the shoes, and admired the magnificent work of art poised carefully in my tiny hands. I proceeded to stuff one foot into each shoe, giddily folding the smooth leather straps over and taking in the view—my little legs, encased in cream-colored tights like tiny little sausages, with two beautiful bookends at the end of each one.

With brand-new shoes on my feet, ready to take on the world, I stood up. I held out the tissue paper still in hand, like a pompom cheering the full celebration of getting my new shoes and learning the new word that came with them.

With outstretched arms, I took a deep breath and proudly announced at the top of my lungs, "*BU-STER!*"

Almost as fast as the word flew out of my mouth, my heart, along with my enthusiasm, plunged into my stomach. For the first time in my life (but certainly not the last), I saw *that* look on my dad's face, then heard the roar and felt the smack that followed.

I vaguely remember my tiny back hitting the wall of the narrow hallway, sliding down it, and crumpling into a pile on the floor. Wide-eyed and stunned, I saw the empty Buster Brown shoe box lying upside-down on the floor. I watched the tissue paper float to the ground as though waving a white flag of surrender in slow motion.

And then it came. My eyes closed shut, my mouth gaped open, I let out the long, silent scream that comes just before a wailing outcry and the bursting dam of tears. After that moment, the rest of the day was a blur. My dad said nothing to me as I sat in the backseat of the car, my tear-streaked face staring out the window, wondering what I had done wrong.

That was the moment when everything in my safe, innocent, happy little world changed. I felt scared, confused, and *wrong*. What I didn't know at the time was how that moment in particular would shape every decision I made for the rest of my life. From that moment on, I would do whatever it took to *never be wrong or rejected again*.

I grew to lose trust in the world around me, in myself, and my relationship to my dad fundamentally changed. And because I thought I had disappointed my dad and felt rejected by him, the stage was set for how I would relate to boys and men later on.

It wasn't until ten years later that I even understood what had happened that day with me and my new shoes.

When I was fourteen years old, I was sitting at the kitchen table with my back to the TV, which my dad was watching intently in the living room. Someone on TV said the word *"buster."* I quickly turned around and, in typical teenage fashion, sarcastically remarked loud enough for everyone to hear how laughable it was for my dad to even think that "buster" was such a bad word, when they used it on daytime television.

Kids of immigrant parents were meant to be seen, not heard. So we were used to our parents getting angry or raising their voices at us. We were used to getting in trouble, and then their never speaking about it again. So, for an entire decade, I had thought *Buster* was a bad word, one I had gotten in trouble for saying out loud as a four-year-old.

My dad turned his head away from the TV for one brief moment, looked at me, and said matter-of-factly, "You didn't say *buster*. You called me a bastard." And then he turned his attention back to the TV.

What? I could not believe my ears. Could it be true that, this whole time, an entire decade, my dad thought I had called him a *bastard?*

For the record, calling a traditional Indian man a bastard is possibly the worst thing you could ever say to him. It indicates that his mother had him out of wedlock, one of the most shameful acts possible in traditional Indian culture. And to insult an Indian man's mother is unforgivable.

Eyes wide, pulse lit, heart pounding, I pounced to my defense at my dad's false accusation.

"Wait. *What?* Are you *SERIOUS?* No. *No*, I did not call you a bastard! I said Buster! *BUSTER!* I had Buster Brown shoes and was so excited I could read the word on the box that I jumped up and yelled it out loud. I mean, really, c'mon, Dad, are you kidding me? How would I even *know* the word *bastard,* when I was four years old?"

Words spewed out of my mouth like fire pouring from a dragon.

He stared at me for a moment, wobbled his head as though he only half believed me (which, incidentally, hurt more than the slap), and then there it was. He did that thing he does with his face when he's just about to tell you that you're *wrong*. He clicked his tongue, furrowed his brow, scrunched up his entire face like he'd just smelled something bad, and said, "Ah, come off it! You said *bastard,* and I felt so bad for hitting you, I even went upstairs and cried."

I just sat there feeling a hundred things all at once. Stunned, incredulous, disappointed, misunderstood, angry, sad, empathetic, guilty, dismissed. I was feeling all the feels as I sat in that confusing place, which I was getting to know so well. The gap.

Looking back now, I can see how preposterous it must have seemed for this traditional Indian man, whose second language was English, to have to listen to his privileged first-world teenage daughter attempt to convince him that she had said *buster,* a word he had probably never even heard of before, instead of *bastard.*

Not only could he not relate to me as a young teenage girl, he had simply zero understanding of what it was like to grow up in a Western world. My dad's teenage years were spent in a refugee camp in New Delhi, eating rationed meals while confined to a hospital bed for almost two years, when he suffered from tuberculosis. So, at an age when I was contemplating which classes I could skip and still pass, my dad had missed two years of school while wondering if he'd ever recover and live long enough to graduate high school.

We were literally worlds apart.

It was unfathomable to my dad that a disgruntled teenager could disrespect their family, especially their parents. He could never imagine complaining about what he *had to* eat for dinner or that he *had to* go to school. For him, it was a privilege to *get to* eat dinner and *get to* go to school; these *"had to"* complaints came from spoiled, first-world brats with first-world problems. And *that* was foreign—and completely unacceptable, by the way—to him. Fair.

But, at fourteen years old, none of this occurred to me. And so, I just sat there in silence.

We never talked about the Buster moment again. And I came to learn that was just the way it was. My dad and I would misunderstand each other often throughout my lifetime, and it was easier to ignore the fact that we didn't understand each other than it was to get curious about the other's perspective. It was easier to sweep feelings under the rug and hope that, one day, they might just disappear. It was easier to avoid the hard conversations and the confusion that came up in the gap rather than to ask questions. So, I learned to keep my "problems" and "complaints" to myself. It was all left unsaid, uncommunicated, and unprocessed.

The gap turned into a chasm.

For an entire decade, my dad thought I had called him a bastard and had even cried about it. For an entire decade, I had decided I did something terribly wrong and had cried about it. But the reality is it wasn't for just a decade. This seemingly harmless misunderstanding created the core wound that impacted my relationship with trust, with myself, with men, and with others for the rest of my life.

As I unearth, understand, and break the core pattern that keeps me small, dim, shackled, under-expressed, and undervalued, it's incredible how one quick moment, based on nothing but a misunderstanding, can change the course of a child's life for decades to come.

I have recounted the many times when immiguilt has paid me a visit over fifty years. I have reflected on the subconscious decisions I made that kept this immiguilt alive and all the conscious decisions I made in order to dismantle it, piece by piece. Writing this book is part of that conscious healing process for me. Because the reality is, we all have a Buster incident.

We all have a moment in time when we lose a piece of ourselves and immediately form a belief about ourselves that will replay itself over and over again in our subconscious. And it's only when we uncover our pattern that we can break it and begin to heal.

I believe that a lot of good came from the Buster incident and the level of growth I've been able to cultivate as a result of it has been transformative. Over the years, I've worked hard to peel away the layers from this moment, excavating my core pattern and the lessons trapped beneath the hurt. I continue to navigate my relationship to accomplishment and failure, getting things right and being wrong. I've learned to let go of playing the victim, harboring resentment, or resisting pain, and I have cultivated forgiveness, resilience, and gratitude instead.

I've been able to redefine my relationship to my parents, my dad, and to men in general. I continue to work toward a more conscious way of communicating, a more empowered way of expressing myself, and a more empathetic way of parenting. Yes, parenting. While I don't have children of my own, I've had to learn to reparent myself. I've learned to care for myself and others in a more mature, compassionate way, giving myself all the things I felt I didn't receive from that Buster moment forward. Had I not done this work for me, as well as redefined my adult relationship with my parents, I could never be the effective caregiver I wish to be for my aging parents, especially in the ways they need me to be now.

As my parents age, I see their old core patterns resurfacing very clearly. And since their cultural background and immigrant circumstance did not allow them to tend to their own childhood wounds, it's now up to me to support them in attempting to resolve theirs in this lifetime. While this may or may not happen, the fact remains that, had I not worked to resolve my own wounds first, I might have been blinded by the pain of the past and unable to recognize that my own wounding stemmed from my parents' unresolved wounding in the first place. And so on.

The cycle of life has come full circle, and as my parents transition into the last phase of their life, they now need me to be understanding and empathetic, acknowledging the fear that comes along with all that. These are also the same things that I needed, and wish I had received, from them, growing up, as I went through my own life transitions.

My goal is to care for my aging parents with a level of patience that's needed to complete this circle well. I see it as the act of building a bridge between us, closing the gap, and allowing immiguilt to finally wash away beneath it. A bridge that spans from me all the way back to my parents' own childhood needs, like feeling heard, nurtured, and validated, so they feel safe enough to finally step out onto the bridge, which has been hanging precariously in the gap between us for so long. And, if I do manage to build a bridge solid enough for all of us to stand on, when my parents are ready to cross over to the other side, they can do so with trust, pride, and peace in their hearts.

It will be the ultimate redemption.

Chapter 4
PAKI

IN 1986, I WAS A smart, confident, creative twelve-year-old girl who felt content at home and did well in school. I had gone to the same Early French Immersion elementary school since kindergarten and finally made it to the senior grade in the school: Grade 6. Yep, we were the twelve-year-old kings and queens of the school. Proud and loud. With a bad case of "senioritis."

We were the oldest kids in the school. The ones with the most experience. The ones who had walked those same hallways since we were five years old. The ones who had earned the right to acquire the biggest lockers, have the biggest desks, and sit at the back of the big yellow school bus!

Not only did we get to sit at the back of the bus, but I somehow thought it was cooler to sit *backward* at the back of the bus, until my arrogant ass was launched straight into the middle of the aisle once, where I not-so-cool-y landed with a loud thump after the driver was forced to slam on the brakes.

One day, after school, a bunch of us Grade-6 kids were sitting at the back of the bus, chatting up a storm, when Alan, one of the shortest boys in our class, stood up in the seat in front of me and announced loudly to the entire bus that he had a joke to tell. Always in the mood for a good laugh, the bus quieted down. We all paused our separate conversations to listen intently to what Alan had to say.

He started, "Okay! A Paki and a—" Stopping abruptly, he swiftly turned around, looked straight at me, and said, "No offense, Serena." Then, like nothing had happened, he turned back around and continued telling the joke.

I didn't hear the rest of the joke. In fact, I didn't hear another word he said. I didn't hear the roar of laughter emanating from the kids at the back of the bus. I didn't hear the bus driver yelling my name when it was my stop. I didn't even hear my mom greet me when I walked through the door.

I had no idea what Alan was talking about. I didn't know what a Paki was. And I didn't know that I was one of them. What I did know was, on that fateful day in Grade 6, I was pointed out as being different from everyone else, and my entire perception of myself changed. I realized that what and who *I* thought I was and what *others* thought I was were not the same thing. I didn't know what a Paki was, but worse, at that moment, I didn't know who I was anymore.

But I was going to find out!

Shortly after the school bus incident, my young ears were peeled for answers to the burning question of, "What am I?" Once I heard someone use the word *Indonesian* and got excited. That's it! That's me! Indo-nese. Half *Indi*an and half Chi*nese*... I must be Indonesian!

I came home from school that day to find my mom in the kitchen as usual, preparing an after-school snack for my sister and me. I plunked my backpack down onto the floor and proudly announced that I finally knew what I was.

SERENA ARORA

"I'm Indonesian!" I exclaimed.

With her standard furrowed brow and pursed lips, which indicated my mom was annoyed, she paused long enough to cast me a confused yet dismissive glance and replied tersely, "No, you're not. Now, hurry up. Eat. Your ballet class starts in forty-five minutes."

Deflated, I picked up my backpack, flung it over my shoulder, and hurried upstairs to get changed—immigrit.

Growing up a mixed-race Asian kid on the Western Canadian Prairies in the seventies and eighties was no small feat. Especially in our quadrant of Calgary. Subtle messages were all around me, influencing and impacting me for decades without my realizing how much. I was often the only non-White kid in the local library, community center, grocery store, or even the mall. I don't remember seeing any non-White store cashiers, librarians, or restaurant servers.

Every single tutor, teacher, and university professor I've ever had from kindergarten through university was White. (I was even the only non-White teacher in two of the three schools where I taught.) Every girl in my entire ballet school, which I attended from ages seven to seventeen years old, was White with either blonde or light-brown hair.

In fact, I didn't realize how much I stuck out like a sore thumb until I saw a picture of our ballet recital one year: my jet-black hair, dark skin, and big, white teeth were all you could see in a row of achromatic pale-pink bodysuits, tights, and skin. All the dolls I played with (Barbies, Strawberry Shortcakes, Cabbage Patch Kids, etc.) had white skin and big blue or green eyes. Being in Early French Immersion in Calgary in the eighties, I was one of only two Indian kids, the only mixed-race kid and the only kid of Chinese descent in all of my classes from kindergarten to Grade 9.

Apart from a handful of cousins on each side of our family unit, I never realized how white my world really was back then. I was just busy being a kid, living my life, and doing kid things in the only world I knew. I didn't actually think I was all that different and had a pretty healthy sense of self. When I was young, I didn't notice the differences—until other people started pointing them out.

My sister and I got called "chocolate bar" or "fudgesicle" (or "poopsicle," if the kids were feeling extra mean) as we got off our elementary school bus in the early years. We'd spend the rest of the walk home in a passionate discussion about what familiar food items were pale enough to call those kids in response, suggestions ranging from vanilla ice cream to marshmallows.

As I grew older, I became more aware and self-conscious of other peoples' judgments about who (and what) they thought I was. When others insinuated I was indeed different and started teasing me about my physical appearance, I started to doubt my worth. It wasn't until I started equating my Asianness to my *looks*, my looks to being *pretty enough*, pretty enough to my *worthiness*, and my worthiness to my *body*, that things took a turn for the worse.

I questioned my own intuition, doubted my decisions, and compared my straight-laced Eastern family upbringing to the increasingly complicated Western world outside of my big house in the 'burbs. Let's just say comparing never ends well.

I had really thick, naturally curly, black South Asian hair that no (White) hairdresser understood how to cut, so I left the salon with helmet hair every time. I found out years later that the kids in my middle school thought I had an oversized head that was too big for my body. Ouch.

SERENA ARORA

My ballet teacher would shout to the entire class, "Headlights forward!" but stare directly at me, the one girl in the class whose "headlights" (a.k.a. hip bones) did not physically tilt forward due to my excessive lumbar curve and bubble butt. A Grade 7 boy called me "Elvis," because my Indian genes had gifted me sideburns. And a boy in Grade 8 called me "Frida" (as in Kahlo), because of my monobrow (again gifted via my Indian genes). And my drama teacher told me I'd never get a lead role, because I would never "look the part."

The worst was when I found out the high school boy to whom I lost my virginity had told his friends, "Serena has a nice body, but I'd have to put a bag over her head,"— insinuating my face wasn't attractive enough for him, if he were to ever sleep with me again. Needless to say, he never got that privilege again.

To add insult to injury, my own straight-shooting, no-sugar-coating immigrant family members actually considered it an act of love to tell me their opinion about my looks as well. For example, when I was twelve, I had the courage to stop hiding my face behind my long hair and got it cut short. I came home, excited to show my traditional Indian dad, only to receive a curled-up nose and a, "It looks *terrible*!" instead.

Or when my older sister and I used words like "shit-brown" to describe the color of our eyes. Or when she barged in on me in the shower to get something when I was thirteen and left, calling out, "Pancakes!" (referring to my flat chest).

Or when I was fifteen and my mom said, "You know, if you had bigger eyes like your sister, you'd be very pretty." (*Hm*, thanks, Mom. I'm pretty sure I didn't get my small eyes from dad.) Or, at age seventeen, when my mom discouraged me from studying journalism at university because "nobody on TV looks like me." (My, how times have changed, Mom.)

I often hid how much all of these comments hurt in the moment. I put on a brave face and sucked it up—*immigrit*. But these seeds were planted in the back of my young mind, covered with layers of scar tissue over time, and still held tightly in my body to this very day.

And while I understand that being teased, called names, and bullied in school is an experience most of us go through to some degree, the thing that affected me the most was having nobody to talk to about it. I didn't have any emotionally mature female adult role models or other mixed-race friends who understood what I was going through. Therapy was not an option for immigrant kids and considered taboo at best and shameful at worst. My White friends couldn't relate to my experience, and I most certainly did not feel safe sharing my experience with my family.

When I was fifteen, I did attempt to articulate how much I felt like I didn't belong to my mom. "I don't think I was meant to be born in Alberta..." I started.

But before I could elaborate, she interrupted me, shouting, *"How dare you say that?* You should be *grateful* we came here! You're so lucky to be born here! God help you..."

Aaaand cue immiguilt. (Oh yeah, did I mention that immiguilt often involved God helping me?)

It was in conversations like these that I learned it wasn't safe to share my emotions. My family seemed to know and show only two emotions: anger and disappointment. Any other emotion wasn't well received. They seemed agitated and uncomfortable whenever I was sad, frustrated, confused, or even excited or too exuberant for their liking. And attempting to process any concern was seen as ungrateful and taken as personal blame for something they did or didn't do.

Let's just say that healthy communication is not our family's strong suit. My family lacks the emotional intelligence, skill, vulnerability, and capacity to discuss complicated emotions and painful experiences. If swept under the (shag) rug, my parents figured, perhaps they'd just disappear.

To complicate matters further, comfort is a value of mine. So, when others seemed uncomfortable around me (which I noticed often), I retracted and did whatever I needed to do in order for their comfort to be restored—immiguilt. And so, I learned to hold in my feelings and navigate them on my own—immigrit.

While this afforded me resilience and independence, it also gnawed at my self-confidence. I questioned my feelings, doubted my intuition, and internalized the dejection. I became an insecure, resentful teenager who lacked support and an inherent sense of belonging. So, in order to save myself yet another disappointment, I got rid of the one thing that kept me feeling different.

I rejected my Asianness.

The problem with rejecting a part of you is you unavoidably end up rejecting *all* of you. And by rejecting this piece of me, I ended up losing myself, piece by piece. To be clear, I did not wake up one day and decide I wasn't Asian anymore. I just subconsciously clung on harder to the things that weren't Asian about me. Like, despite there being quite a few South Asians in my high school, I still befriended White girls who looked the exact opposite of me: blonde hair, blue eyes, and red lips. All my friends at school were White, all my friends out of school were White, and even all my "wannabe friends" on TV were White.

I related to White people more than I did with the Chinese kids in Chinese school or even my own flesh-and-blood family members who had grown up in India and Singapore. It's like my drama teacher said, I just "didn't look the part."

I'm pretty sure I've never quite looked the part for anything in this audition called life. With a Chinese mom, and Indian dad, English as my native tongue, and being fluent in French, I can understand how confusing it must have been for people who were looking in from the outside. So confusing, in fact, that people literally stopped what they were doing and stared at me.

I got stared at a lot in my late teens and early twenties. I'm talking full-on brazen stares. From across cafés and restaurants, in stores, on the subway, even driving my car, alone or with a group of friends… Wherever and whenever. And mostly by middle-aged White men. As an insecure teen and sassy twenty-something, I stared right back at them, gave them dirty looks, ignored them, or just straight-up asked them what the hell they were staring at. And that's when I heard the slow, apologetic signature stutter that would play on repeat for years to come: "Oh, um, yeah, er, sorry… *Uhhhhh…* Can I ask… *ummm… What are you?"*

"What are you?" has been the last-round Jeopardy question of my entire life. I've been asked that question more times than I can count, and believe it or not, I still don't have a very good answer. I just stood there, dumbfounded

and slightly embarrassed about being so rude to them. Depending on how I felt that day, I'd answer anything from, "A human being" to "Guess" to the actual answer they were looking for.

I get it now. They were genuinely curious. My "look" intrigued them. I imagine they had likely traveled or even lived abroad at some point and were attempting to place my face and ethnicity. Since I can pass for so many things, I can only imagine what was going through their minds as they wracked their brain, hoping to get it right. "Asian? Latin American? Indigenous?"

Sometimes, if I listened carefully, I could hear the soothing voice of *Planet Earth's* David Attenborough playing in their heads: "What is this exotic creature doing all the way up here in the vast plains of our North American tundra? And what on Earth will she find up here to *eat*?"

The unfortunate part was I was just as confused as they were. I consistently felt bothered, hopeless, and unclear about who I was and my place in this world. I wanted to feel a sense of belonging so badly, but I kept failing to find it anywhere I went in the world. In India, they thought I was Japanese. In Malaysia, they thought I was Thai. In Australia, they thought I was Aboriginal. In America, they thought I was Mexican. And in Africa, they just pointed at me and yelled, "Sushiland!"

When all the subtle and not-so-subtle messages that I received in different ways, by different people, and in different places, proved too much for my young, impressionable mind, I decided I was indeed different. And, until I wasn't anymore, I would never belong.

And so, I did what any lost, ill-equipped teenager would do. I sought out people and things who I believed would validate my enough-ness. And, while some insecure teens turn to smoking, alcohol, drugs, or other substances to numb the discomfort and pain, I didn't. I hated the smell of cigarettes from a young age, didn't like the effects of alcohol, and stayed far away from drugs.

So, instead, I turned to boys.

Chapter 5
WHORES & PROSTITUTES

MY TIRES SQEALED as I peeled around the corner of the cul-de-sac toward our family home. It was almost 2:00 a.m. on a Saturday night. I jammed the pedal down, speeding up to the house as though saving half a second would actually make a difference at this point, and rounded the curb before lurching to a halt on our driveway.

I was a sixteen-year-old high school senior, and I was late for my curfew. Again. In school, I had a decent overall grade-point average, but I held a steady failing grade in the subjects of self-worth, security, and self-image. I'd earned this grade over time and sustained it by choosing to hang out with a group of boys with whom I would never feel "enough." What can I say? It felt familiar. And, of course, these boys saw my insecurities a mile away, preyed on my warped sense of worth, and used it to their advantage.

My image of myself back then is as a disheveled princess who lost her crown years ago. Desperate for love, she now finds herself on her hands and knees, searching for it in the scrapyard of humanity, scrounging for any pathetic crumbs dropped by those teenage boys to keep her coming back for more. I not only allowed them to treat me this way, I was a sucker for punishment—immigrit.

If I'm being honest, there was nothing special about these boys. They weren't popular, overly kind, or good looking (my brutally honest mom even nicknamed one of them "bootface"). My girlfriends used to plead with me, "You're way better than that asshole!" or "What the hell do you see in that guy, anyway?" or "He's such a jerk to you." or "You're beautiful, Serena, go find someone who thinks that, too."

But my self-perception was painfully distorted. I didn't believe them for the simple reason that I had stopped believing in myself long before that. This distorted view I had of myself, along with my deep yearning for touch and affection, took me down a dark, sordid spiral where I relied on boys to validate my worth. It's a hard pill to swallow, knowing that, while drugs were a definite *no* for me, the addiction to feeling loved kept me willfully blind in the delusional depths of teenage darkness.

I was almost two hours late for my curfew, and I had never been out this late before. I had purposely broken my curfew because I'd been with the guy I had pined over for a year. ("That asshole," as my friends referred to him.) For whatever reason, sixteen-year-old Serena had selected him as "the one" and, that night, she had finally "won" the one. Or so she thought. While my naïve interpretation was of "winning," I couldn't shake the feeling that I had lost so much more than my virginity that night. I wasn't wrong.

For just a brief moment before getting out, I sat in my car, reflecting on this strange experience. A rite of passage into adulthood on the one hand, and a courageous act of vulnerability that had transformed my relationship to my body, on the other. For me, though, personally, a total mind fuck.

I quickly snuck around the side of our house, walked into the garage, and cracked the door open as quietly as I could. Light streamed into the garage. Damn. The kitchen light was on. Which meant Mom had decided to wait up for me.

It was always Mom. During the week, Dad worked long hours as a corporate controller for one of the richest men in the city at the time, and then managed his rental properties in the evenings and on weekends. So he wasn't home a lot, and when he was, his mind seemed elsewhere. As was typical of Indian fathers, and maybe most dads back in those days, he wasn't involved in our school or extracurricular activities or privy to our whereabouts most of the time. So, when I came home late, he usually didn't even find out about it until the next day.

Not tonight.

I slipped off my shoes, took a deep breath, and prepared for my mom's wrath. At sixteen, I had already been bigger and taller than my mom for years, so running after me with a flyswatter was no longer an option. Her fury against my teen rebellion was expressed through a constant stream of scolding, interspersed with lip pursing, fist pumping, and full-body pacing, until she got it out of her system. Eventually, she'd run out of steam and tell me to go to my room. Kind of like Shrek watching Lord Farquaad have a temper tantrum.

When I walked into the kitchen, my mom was perched at her usual spot at the kitchen table, reading her book. "Oh. Hey, Mom, you still up?" I asked casually in that innocent lilt every teenager naïvely thinks dupes our parents.

Silence. Without looking up from her book, she pursed her lips, her signature move that let us know she was about to blow.

She didn't.

Her pursed lips slowly parted and, through gritted teeth, she said six words in staccato, emphasizing the first and last syllable of each word. "Wait. Until. Your. Dad. Comes. Down."

And then I heard it. Heavy footsteps making their way down the long, upstairs hallway and scrambling down the stairs. Hurried and on a mission. An angry mission. My dad appeared from around the corner in his rumpled pajamas and a wide-eyed, worried, but bordering on rage look on his face. I had grown to know that look far too well at that point in my life, too.

He leaned in toward me and shouted, *"Do you know what time it is?"*

Keeping a casual tone, I responded, "Uh, no, actually, I don't. What time is it?"

"It's two o'clock in the bloody morning!" he roared.

Then, he did something I'll never forget. He reached behind my head, grabbed my long hair at the scruff of my neck, and yanked it down. I dropped to my knees. "Only whores and prostitutes are out at this hour!" he yelled. I closed my eyes.

The shame and guilt that washed over me in that very moment could have bowled me over ten times harder than his grip on my hair. It didn't matter whether or not he knew I had lost my virginity that night. I knew. I knelt there on the kitchen floor, drowning in a tsunami of immiguilt. And in one of the most vulnerable times in a young girl's life, this experience defined my relationship to the most intimate part of myself: my sexuality. On my knees, feeling ashamed and unworthy, guilty and dirty, a despicable disappointment.

I didn't hear anything else that was said before my dad clambered back upstairs.

I took a breath, opened my eyes, slowly got up from the floor, mumbled goodnight to my mom, and went upstairs to bed.

In Asian culture, talking about sex, sexuality, or even sensuality is taboo. Public displays of affection between romantic partners are considered rude, lewd, and disrespectful. There's no public hand-holding, no kissing, and absolutely, unequivocally no sex. As a side note, I seriously have no idea how Asian countries are the most populous countries in the world.

It's particularly uncommon (or non-existent, in my case) to see your parents display any kind of physical affection toward each other. In fifty years, I have never seen my parents hold hands, kiss, or show physical or verbal affection of any kind to each other. And, while this is understood by children throughout Asia, especially in traditional Asian families, kids of immigrants live a whole other (confusing) reality. I'd see my friends' parents openly hug, kiss, sleep in the same bedroom, and even smack each other on the ass sometimes, and I started questioning what love looked like in a romantic partnership or, worse, if my parents actually loved each other.

Love is another complicated topic I've had to dissect over the years. For me, love was an unspoken rule that nobody made reference to, articulated, or acted upon. As a kid, I knew I was loved, but I don't remember ever getting hugged (especially by my Chinese mom) or told I was loved. Love was understood. My parents loved us, and their immigrit told us this every single day.

Romantic love, however, felt like a very different story to me. It was a confusing story that I didn't understand and nobody dared to tell. This taboo topic was part of a storybook that lived on a secret shelf somewhere in our home, accumulating dust. So, when I became a teenager, I had questions. I needed to find the book, grab it off the shelf, dust it off, and thumb through the unfamiliar story, searching for answers on my own.

As my body began to change and grow, so did my confusion about relationships, romance, my body, and, yes, sex. I didn't understand much about the human body, how it worked, or what all these changes meant, let alone learn about any new species of birds and bees. There was no sex education in school at that time, and our family conversations were limited to three topics: food, finances, and fractions. And so, I was left to fend for myself when it came to figuring out acne, mood swings, and tampons. The words *sex* or *sexuality* have never been spoken in our home. Ever. Even as an adult. And, to this day, my dad will quickly change the channel or leave the room if a (barely) racy scene comes on TV or appears in a movie.

As an adolescent who did not yet understand the concept of healthy physical touch and who had not witnessed or really received it myself, growing up, I craved it deeply. Unfortunately for me, I was also left to navigate this feeling and curiosity all on my own. It was a confusing and complicated ride.

I didn't know it at the time, but when I heard that the guy I had lost my virginity to told his friends he would have to put a bag over my head, that confusion turned to shame.

I decided I would never feel shame like that again. So, I decided to stop *feeling* altogether. Instinctively, I shut off my heart and shut down my mind (and, consequently, any discernment I might have had around boys and sex), and I operated solely from the place where I had always felt the safest... my body.

Cut off from my emotions, my body became the main driver of my decisions. After many heartless and mindless acts, looking for love in all the wrong places, I learned to separate my body from my feelings, my thoughts, and my own needs and desires. My body became a source of both pride and shame, accomplishment and resentment, a means to an end, and a shameful end to a means. There were times when I respected, nurtured, and upheld it on a pedestal. Other times, disrespected, abused, and gave it away.

After I had sex only one time, was indirectly compared to whores and prostitutes on the same night, and then heard afterward that the guy I'd broken curfew for would "have to put a bag over my head," a switch inside of me flipped.

I realized I actually had something that could be used to hurt others more than they could hurt me. I couldn't control what anyone said or believed about me or my body, but I could control them *with* my body. It was the ultimate revenge.

I used my body to seduce and reduce, to attract and attack, to seek external validation and perceived "love." I used my body as a tool to get what I wanted until I didn't want it anymore. My body got me into relationships, into jobs, into places, and into trouble. And sex, for me, after that fateful night kneeling on the kitchen floor, became purely transactional.

My tool became my weapon.

Chapter 6
WINONA

AS SO MANY YOUNG people would agree, I'd say being a teenager was probably the most confusing time of my life. Attempting to inhabit a body that was constantly changing while navigating mental, emotional, and physical growing pains, I fell into the same traps of insecurity, discomfort, and shame that so many teenage girls face during adolescence. So much rapid transformation occurs within such a short period (pun intended) of time.

On top of all that, in my immigrant family, emotional and mental wellbeing were so far down the priority totem pole, it was practically underground. And unearthing your feelings was risky business. There wasn't one adult in my circle who could relate to what I was going through or could just listen without judging me or offering unsolicited advice. As a result, I spent a lot of time in my head, trying to make sense of it all on my own.

Not only did I live in my mind, I was a late bloomer, physically. I stayed painfully skinny until I was about fourteen years old, at which time I started to get hips, boobs, an ass, and my period. While some girls seemed to wake up one morning at twelve, fully developed, my body decided to take its sweet time.

SERENA ARORA

The changes felt awkward. My breasts began as hard, tender buds behind my nipples, which were uncomfortable at best and painful at worst. When I was nine, my mom had a benign tumor removed from her breast, so when I complained to her about the pain in my chest at fourteen and she discovered hard masses of tissue behind my nipples, she feared the worst. So, like all good immigrant mothers, she decided to bring it up in front of *my dad* one evening, insisting I show him, so *he* could decide if we should be concerned at all. (I can practically hear the women reading this cringe).

That moment was not only mortifying for me, it was equally torturous for my dad, a traditional immigrant man and an accountant, no less. He had no clue how to handle the sensitive situation his prepubescent daughter was going through. Clearly just as uncomfortable with it as I was, my dad forced a quick glance at my chest and mumbled something about a walk-in clinic before turning his attention back to the safety of the television.

At the walk-in clinic, I was, once again, asked to show a random male doctor my buds. Humiliated by my first bumpy (pun intended again) experience with puberty, entering womanhood felt unnecessarily traumatic to me—especially when the doctor told my mom that this was a "perfectly normal" part of the development process. *Just perfect.* I think I preferred pancakes.

Despite the awkwardness of puberty, I've always been fascinated by the human body. I spent a lot of time moving mine, using it for all sorts of activities (did I mention the word *extracurricular*?), which gave me a sense of pride and accomplishment. When I was younger, I felt the most at home when I was in my body. It moved it in all kinds of ways that made me feel strong, flexible, and intrinsically safe and protected. I understood it.

In fact, my body was one of few things in my life that I did understand. I relied on and believed in it fully, and, up to that point, it had yet to disappoint me. It moved easily, danced gracefully, bent effortlessly, and jumped infinitely. It responded to my demands with ease, and I felt deeply connected to it. It was like a finely-tuned instrument that played a seasoned musician, rather than the other way around.

My body could have been on a podium, winning awards, but something other than my body held me back from going there. The doubt, shame, and fear of failure that was engrained in my (apparently oversized, according to the middle-school crowd) head. Immiguilt held a firm grip on my mind, the belief that I was not worthy of winning. At least not first place, that is.

Second, however, was a place I knew all too well. Second-born, second-generation, and second-guessing. It goes back to that Buster Brown moment. The pride I'd felt for reading that word was extinguished by the painful wave of doubt and confusion that followed. I decided, in that brief yet impactful Buster moment, I would never risk taking the leap into the spotlight ever again. And that spotlight was me.

I learned at that moment that my light could be too blinding for some people, so much so that they cannot see me for who I truly am, including my own dad. So, I began to dim my own light so others could shine instead. I learned it was much safer and more comfortable being in second place and letting others win and take the spotlight.

A stark example of this occurred in seventh grade. My gym teacher and track coach, Ms. Lawrence, saw me run and was determined to prove a point.

During gym class, we all stood in the hallway in pairs, preparing to race the 50-meter sprint. All eyes were on Alli, the "fastest" girl in our grade, who was standing at the start of the line.

Ms. Lawrence walked over to the gaggle of kids standing behind Alli, looked around, and locked eyes on me. She grabbed me by the shoulder with one hand, pulled me up beside Alli, and announced, "I want you two to race."

There was an audible gasp from the crowd of kids as she nodded at me, half smiling. I still remember the stunned look on Alli's face as Ms. Lawrence spun around, walked back to the end of the hallway, and raised her arm straight up in the air, her thumb poised on the stopwatch.

My heart pounded out of my chest as we lined up. I grabbed the edges of the doorway to brace myself and waited for the whistle.

Ready! Set! Tweeeeeeeetttt!

I stared straight ahead, pumped my arms and legs, and sprinted down the hall the only way I knew how. We were almost at the finish line when I caught a glimpse of Alli out of the corner of my eye. I was ahead of her. But just before the finish line, something inside me held me back, and Alli crossed the finish line first.

I knew it, and Ms. Lawrence knew it, too: I had *let* her win. Ms. Lawrence looked at me with a disappointed yet knowing glance. In her heart, she believed I could have won. The problem was, I didn't—immiguilt.

I often held myself back. Whether out of fear of failure, the weight of expectations, or the engrained belief that even first place would never be "enough," something stopped me from stepping into the spotlight.

While I loved being in my body, my looks had also attracted a lot of negative attention since I was young. From people wondering what I was to making off-color remarks, judgments, and harmful comparisons by peers and family members, I developed a distorted perception of self and hid. But when I went through the physical changes of adolescence, I started to receive a very different kind of attention—boys gave me approving glances, and girls complimented me. This shift caught me off guard and became a source of confusion for me once again.

While my body had blossomed, my teenage mind remained in damage control. I was still jaded by judgments and crippled by criticism, leaving my self-esteem so low, I couldn't discern between positive and negative attention anymore. I'd spent so many years trying to shrink myself that now, when I could have embraced the positive attention and used it to eradicate self-doubt, instead I retreated into the safety of my comfort zone—second place.

I was starved for affection and attention, but the attention I received was rarely from people who valued me for who I truly was. Instead, my second-place status attracted second-class boys who saw me as a conquest and reduced my value to something superficial. I became the very thing I feared: a tool to fulfill someone else's desires, not my own. And, sadly, I was perfectly fine with coming in second.

When I look back at how my high school experience played out, I see my core pattern. I learned very young that proving my worth to my parents meant accomplishing a task, reaching a goal, or "winning" a challenge. However, since I didn't receive much praise for achieving these wins, I instinctively took on bigger and more challenging tasks. The greater the challenge, the harder I worked to prove I could "win." Perhaps then, I'd be praised or feel a sense of accomplishment for my hard work.

The accolade never came. In fact, the opposite was true. I was criticized for being "too loud," "too big," and "too passionate," because being too much of anything was considered disrespectful and *wrong*. It made my immigrant family uncomfortable. With that, I ended up feeling stuck in my belief that, no matter what I did, or didn't do, I would never be enough.

I then created the excuse that "winning" first place would garner too much uncomfortable attention, and since I already had an aversion to discomfort, I settled for second best. What started as an innocent craving for attention transformed into an unconsciously perverted sense of pursuit and accomplishment, which proved deeply damaging—especially when this strategy was applied to boys (and boys in men's clothing).

The strategy went something like this: I picked an average guy who I believed would never consider pursuing me (a.k.a. the challenge). He became the target of my affection, attention, and desire... to *win*. I would then pursue him and test whether I'd be rejected or accepted. The more he rejected me, the greater the challenge, and the more I wanted to "win" his affection.

If he rejected me, that was one thing, but when his mother rejected me, too, it brought the challenge to a whole other level. It upped the ante. Not only did I place my worthiness on the level of the challenge, I was going to win no matter how challenging it was. Watch me!—*immigrit*.

And that's when the "win at all costs" girl within me reared her ugly head. You know the one. The devilishly relentless girl who goes out of her way to stand in yours, gets laser-focused, and uses sophisticated manipulation tactics she has developed over time and with experience, to *win*. Let's call her Winona. (Apologies in advance to any Winonas reading this.)

Winona lives in my head and will do whatever it takes to win at all costs. When she appears inside my brilliant mind, all rationale is out the door. Disguised as an experienced, opinionated, know-it-all, she offers unsolicited advice and controls the situation by bulldozing everyone and everything in her way with her big yellow bus. To win the argument, the prize, the guy, no matter what.

We all have a Winona. She presents as controlling, coercing, forcing, fixing, demanding, nagging, protecting, saving, blaming, pushing, insisting, worrying, pleasing, perfecting, and pursuing. Winona represents my disintegrated feminine energy. She shows up whenever she thinks I'm unsafe or in need of proving my worth. She's my fierce protector, preserver, and warrior who wants the best for me, but in the worst way. She jumps into the driver's seat and takes over in an attempt to protect me from getting hurt again, like when I was four years old, back up against the wall, the upside-down Buster Brown shoebox at my feet.

She never wants to see me like that again, except Winona is, herself, a hurt little girl at her core. So, if she's not heeded in the moment, she becomes a shameless, needy toddler who amps up her game in full temper-tantrum mode. Winona has had a lot of practice throwing temper tantrums in my head over the years. In fact, she's so practiced at it, most times she sneaks up on me. Unpleasant to say the least. And, if one isn't careful, her aggressiveness is easy to believe, feel sorry for, and sometimes even admire. Winona lacks maturity and empathy, but there's one thing that Winona lacks most of all: discernment. And that's where the trouble begins.

As long as the boy (and his mom) kept rejecting me, Winona continued the pursuit. And if I did manage to "win" him or if he did or said something to make me feel accepted in some way, I'd feed off those crumbs until I was humiliated and hurt enough for Winona to realize she hadn't gotten what she wanted. And so, she flipped the script.

As soon as Winona won the guy, she discarded him like an old, stained, outdated sofa and went on to the next pursuit. No waving her prize high over her head on a podium. No celebration. No accolade. Because there was nothing to celebrate. The intention wasn't pure, the outcome was forced, and feelings were never reciprocated. But Winona was relentless. She had her eye on the prize and was focused on the challenge of the chase, looking for love in all the wrong places. Winona made terrible decisions for me until she won and then sprinted off to find her next challenge, while I was left to clean up the mess she had left behind.

As you can imagine, Winona got stronger, more powerful, flexible, and skilled as time went on—the ultimate story-maker and shape-shifter. Whenever Winona was around, I was having an out-of-body experience. And when I'm out of my body, I'm far from that safe, reliable place I know. Nothing good has ever come from me being out of my body or from Winona taking charge. Every time I made an out-of-body decision, Winona felt as though she had "won," but there I was, the real loser in the situation, feeling shitty about myself for "winning" a guy who was there for all the wrong reasons.

Twisted, I know.

Wait. It gets worse.

The *nice* guys didn't win with Winona. As a teenager, I had plenty of chances to be with nice guys. The nice guys were nice looking, had nice mothers, used nice words and gestures for me, and treated me, well, nicely. Nice guys were everywhere around me. They sat behind me in class, ran next to me on the track team, and ate next to me in the cafeteria. The ones who didn't go to my school hung out with me after school because they *wanted to*. These were the guys with whom I was free to be myself, 100% the real me, the confident, smart, charismatic girl I call *Serena fucking Arora*.

Winona was nowhere to be found when I was with these guys. She didn't need to be. Serena fucking Arora didn't need Winona's fierce protection and grit with these guys, because we both knew I was in my own body, feeling safe, secure, and free.

But here's the catch. If any of those nice guys were attracted to me, Winona would suddenly appear out of nowhere and flip a switch. A trap door would open up beneath them, and they'd immediately drop deep into the friend zone. If they already liked me, that meant there was no challenge at all. And then, what would I have to prove? Nothing. You see, keeping the nice guys at arm's length while I pursued the jerk who could possibly reject me was a greater challenge and far more appealing to me... well, to Winona. And during my late teens then well into adulthood, Winona was definitely in the driver's seat. I let her drive the bus for years and it landed me flat on my backwards ass in the middle of the aisle every single time. Ugh. The epitome of ass backwards. <sigh>

There's a lot of shame attached to the pattern of wanting to win at all costs and in reflecting on my sexual experiences and relationships, in general. So, I knew, in order to heal this part of me and my relationship to my body, I had to face Winona head on.

To acknowledge, forgive, and release the shameful parts of me associated with my body was at the heart of my healing path. Only by remembering and acknowledging these unglamorous experiences first, and then cutting the cord that kept me tied to them, was I able to dissolve the power they still had over me.

I had been dragging them behind me on a hook, each one heavier than the last. As I trudged through life with this heavy load, I'd allowed them to influence my next steps. Buried in shame and exhaustion, it was nearly impossible for my tired body to keep moving forward with ease. And so, I did something that Winona would never do.

I let them off the hook.

I let every person, place, and pursuit connected to my body and sexual past off the hook, so I could free myself from Winona's wrath once and for all. I let them off the hook so I no longer associated my sexuality with shame and unworthiness. I let them off the hook so I could reprogram my relationship to touch.

I let them off the hook so my body understood she was deeply worthy of expressing her desires and showing up just as she is.

I let them off the hook so I could see sex as transformational, instead of transactional.

I let them off the hook so I could remind myself that physical touch and sex can be healthy, healing, vulnerable, and self-soothing.

I let them off the hook so I could free myself of the weightiness of my sexual past and foster a healthy desire for connection and intimacy.

I let them off the hook so I could spend more time in the embodied safety and security of my embodied, integrated feminine energy (the complete opposite of Winona).

It hasn't been easy, reflecting on this part of my life, but part of the healing process for me has been the attempt to connect the dots of my past experiences, which I've come to discover created the perfect storm for what followed. For it is only after we reach a certain age that we can look back and see the common thread we've woven throughout our childhood, teenage years, and into adulthood. Only then can we connect the dots of decisions we made and trace them back to one end of the long thread. And only if we're courageous enough to pull on that thread can the whole thing unravel, revealing the hidden lessons inside. Then, we can finally unwrap and heal the tightly sealed package that we thought we had put away forever.

In my unpacking process, I traced the thread back to its very beginning. Birth. My birth experience is positioned to be an undeniable source of the missing link in my life: physical touch. While some might argue it began even before I was born, craving physical touch has been the driving force behind many of my decisions and something I've searched for my entire life.

Being denied physical touch at birth, then lacking it during childhood, misusing it throughout my teenage years, and then searching for it in adulthood are all karmic circumstances that have led me down a long and winding path in search for true and profound intimacy.

I was born by C-section in the seventies in North America, when mothers were still fully sedated and fathers weren't present; therefore, I had no skin-to-skin contact with my parents. Not only was I born by Caesarian, I was immediately put in an incubator, where I breathed, ate, and slept for the first four weeks of my life. The doctors said this was due to my small size.

Sure, I was just under five pounds. But I was a healthy, hairy, alert little thing who was past full term. I was just… Asian. A five-pound baby is actually quite normal by Asian standards, especially since my mom barely weighed a hundred pounds soaking wet and pregnant. But, being born in North America in the seventies meant none of that was a consideration. I was simply labeled as too small and put directly into an incubator.

Touch was monitored, permitted only through holes in the incubator with gloved hands. I wasn't breastfed. I wasn't even named until I left the hospital, so the tag on the incubator read, "Girl Arora." It's no wonder I craved touch and belonging.

I often think about that tiny, helpless, innocent newborn with the hairy forehead who couldn't advocate for herself. I sometimes imagine her muted cries from behind closed walls, more effortful than the attention she received. Pinched and prodded, her tiny arms and legs flailing, begging for a nurturing naked touch, while her tiny lips gaped open in search of her mother's soothing breast.

She might have wanted to say, "Wait! No! Don't put me in here. I'm fine. I'm not small. I just need physical touch, deep connection, and intimate nurturing. Mommy! Where's my mommy? Who do I *belong* to?!"

I feel that little Girl Arora has been fighting to be heard and understood her whole life. That primal need for her body to be held, nurtured, and nourished was all she wanted and something she deeply deserved. And while her parents loved her, they were immigrants who wouldn't dare question or doubt the competence of the First World, which they knew very little about at the time.

Girl Arora longed for touch, intimacy, connection, and the comfort of suckling on the nipple of her mother's bare breast. This is something I never got; therefore, I settled for second best—a milk substitute, if you will, and I've yearned for the real thing for as long as I can remember.

When I was in my late thirties, I received a few whispers from the Universe that encouraged me to start exploring my birth experience. I began to tap into what little Girl Arora wanted, needed, and craved. Receiving nurturing physical touch remains my love language today, and the adult me realizes it's my responsibility to provide little Girl Arora with this ultimate act of self-love.

The first sign from the Universe came when I was visiting my good friend who was studying to be a midwife. While taking a tour of her birthing center, I walked past an empty incubator that literally took my breath away. Forced to stop and catch my breath, I put one hand on my chest and one hand on the machine beside me.

Not knowing what it was at first, I felt a beckoning from deep inside this strange machine, as though something inside it was crying out to me. I stared at the empty incubator, placed my other hand on it, and closed my eyes. The calling was so strong, like nothing I had ever felt before.

My girlfriend, who hadn't realized I had stopped, came back to the room and asked me if I was okay.

"Um," I asked slowly, "is this an incubator?"

She nodded. "Yes. Have you ever seen one before?"

"Not in thirty-eight years," I replied.

I believe in higher powers and signals from the Universe, and this pull was too powerful to ignore. I knew there was something deeper I needed to explore here.

The next whisper came a couple of years later, during a breathwork session at a yoga festival. I had done breathwork before, but this time it was different.

My breath was hollow, as though I was surrounded by glass walls and a glass ceiling. (Oh, the symbolism.) I suddenly got a visual of me inside an incubator. Breathing, crying, breathing, crying. Nobody hearing me, breathing, crying louder.

And then, my eyes shut, I felt a naked hand touching the bare skin on my shoulder. Somebody had finally heard little Girl Arora. I softened beneath the hand, opened my mouth to let out a silent scream from the back of my throat, and allowed tears to flow through me like salty ocean waves. Tides lapping repeatedly against my shores, cleansing me free of the shame, the immiguilt, and the tight grip that Winona had had on me all those years.

Chapter 7
WRONG SIDE OF THE TRACKS

IN 1996, I WAS A free-spirited, twenty-two-year-old, brand-new university graduate, and I'd accepted my first French immersion teaching job in Deer Lake, a little town in northern Alberta. After packing up a few of my belongings, I drove up north and moved into my new apartment, sight unseen.

Going away for university had been a good decision for me. I began testing my relationship to comfort, to see how far I could take it. By the time I graduated, I wasn't afraid of trying something new, changing apartments, relationships, even universities for an exchange program in my third year. I had become innately resourceful, learned to adapt quickly to my new environment and started to trust that whatever the Universe had in store for me was exactly what I needed at the time, even if it was uncomfortable. *Especially* if it was uncomfortable—immigrit.

I walked around my new apartment, wiped my sweaty forehead with the back of my hand, and plunked my butt down onto the single futon that doubled as a couch in my living room. I stared at the half-unpacked boxes of random comfort items spilling out onto the living room floor: my favorite mug, clothes hangers, towels, bamboo cutting board, lemongrass-scented candle, and a plethora of CDs.

I sighed. It had taken me seven hours to drive from my hometown up to this northern town on the lake with a U-Haul trailer attached to the back of my green Honda SUV. I had never been this far north. I had also never lived in a small town before, let alone a town located 130 miles away from a major city. I'm embarrassed to say I didn't know people even lived this far outside of cities.

My family had never really ventured in this direction on our road trips, either. Those family trips, taken with the seats down in the back of my dad's faux-wood-paneled station wagon, had generally been drives out west to Banff or British Columbia, or out east to Ontario and Quebec, or down south, to the United States.

Aptly named for its natural lakes, parks, and wildlife, Deer Lake is where people enjoy hiking, fishing, and camping. If there's one thing White North Americans love to do, it's go camping. For Asian immigrants, nothing could be less appealing. Especially for millions of South Asian immigrants like my dad, who grew up in a refugee camp, lived in a tent, hauled water, cooked over a fire, and was made to ration food at a young age. Forced to camp throughout his childhood due to the Partition of India, he worked way too hard in his adult life to make his family go through the same traumatic experience as he'd had. Needless to say, camping was never suggested while I was growing up.

At the time I moved there for my first teaching job, the town of Deer Lake had a population of just over 2,700 people. To put it into perspective, there were more kids in my Calgary high school than there were in that entire town.

We had only one main street with traffic lights. It was lined with a random smattering of businesses: a local café, a Subway restaurant, a candy store, a grocery store, two bars, two banks, a Dollar Store, a hotel, a gas station, and a Radio Shack.

While the aesthetics of the town left much to be desired, the natural beauty surrounding it was a hidden gem. It was home to one of the biggest lakes in the region, gorgeous provincial parks and conservation areas, abundant big game and wildlife, a UNESCO world heritage site, and home to the second Muslim mosque ever built in Canada. So, I found this little town piquing my curiosity at every turn, especially while observing the ways in which people lived. They often drove with only one hand on the steering wheel, because the other hand was used to wave constantly to someone they knew. Locks on doors of cars and homes seemed pointless, as they were rarely used. And my Honda SUV felt like a foreign tiny clown car in a town filled with domestic, diesel pickup trucks.

On my first day there, as the sun was just about to set, I heard loud voices coming from outside. I slid open the patio doors to my balcony and walked outside. I lived in the corner unit on the top floor of a small, four-story apartment building. When I looked around, I could see an identical replica of my building to the north, an empty field in front of me, and train tracks that ran along the south side of the building.

I tracked the voices to an area behind the train tracks and spotted a group of five young teenagers standing in the tall grass. They were all huddled together, as if protecting one another from the wind. My emergency assessment and fitness-instructor CPR skills kicked in. *What's going on? Are they okay? Do they look hurt?* I scanned the surroundings for broken electrical poles, downed power lines, and fires. And there it was. *Fire*!

I ran inside to grab my phone, my finger poised in perfect emergency preparedness. But then, laughter interrupted my fingers' cadence. I stepped back onto the balcony and saw the kids jumping around the fire, hooting and hollering in pure joy, with a wild, primal sense of accomplishment, like early humans at the dawn of civilization who had just discovered fire. I realized that they had set the overgrown grass on fire on purpose, for their own entertainment, and it was not an emergency at all.

When one of them looked up and noticed me standing on the balcony, he gestured, and they all scattered in different directions, leaving behind a small puff of black smoke. *Those punks*, I thought. *They better not be my students.* They most certainly were, by the way.

Just then, my phone rang. *Hmm.* It was an unknown number from Calgary. I answered.

"Hello?"

"Hi, is this Serena Arora?"

"Yes, it is," I affirmed.

"Hi, Serena, this is Renee from Greentree Elementary School in Calgary. How are you?"

"Um... Yes, hi. I'm well, thanks. How are you?"

"I'm fine, thanks. I'm phoning to offer you a teaching position that just came available at our school starting next week. We'd like to hire you."

My stomach dropped. I had applied to the Calgary Board of Education as soon as I graduated. My first choice had been to find an opportunity to live and work in my hometown, be close to immediate and extended family members, and work in the biggest city and school district in the province.

I couldn't believe it. If only I had waited a few more months before saying yes to the first offer I got. Like I said, though, I tended to act quickly and jump at any opportunity that presented itself.

I sat there, staring at the phone.

"Hello? Are you still there?" I heard on the other end.

"Oh, yes, hi, Renee. I'm still here." As much as I wanted to yell, *"YES! I'll take it!"* into the phone, my immiguilt kicked in. I had already made a commitment and signed a contract with the school district in this little northern town. Reneging on it at this point would have meant leaving people in a lurch and causing potential disappointment. My immiguilt would simply not allow for that.

"Oh… uh… wow…" I stammered. "I'm honored, and, gosh, as much as I'd love to say yes, I've already accepted another full-time job in another school district."

"Ah, okay. I thought as much. It's really getting down to the wire. I wish you well and the best of luck in your teaching career," she replied.

It felt so final. After a few other pleasantries, I put the phone down and my heart sank with it.

As disappointed as I was, I also still believed I was in Deer Lake for a reason and, as I mentioned earlier, trusted that what the Universe had in store for me was exactly what I needed. I can now say with certainty that it was.

I sat on my balcony and stared at the burnt patch of grass behind the train tracks. I had literally found myself on the wrong side of the tracks. *Hmm*, I thought. My mom had always warned us about places like these. She had intentionally distracted her kids with all sorts of activities to keep us from getting lured to the other side of the tracks.

She was right. I did end up being exposed to a lot of things I hadn't heard about before, while living in Deer Lake, and I also came to discover that the other side of the tracks wasn't as bad as my mom had made us believe. In only two years living in Deer Lake, I rode quads, Ski-Doos, boats, lawn tractors, combines, and big trucks across frozen lakes. I attempted cross-country skiing, waterskiing, fishing, snowshoeing, golf, curling, and, yes, even camping. I learned the importance of checking cistern levels, how to prime a water pump (because I failed to do the previous activity often enough), how to filet a fish, and, of course, how to build a fire.

I discovered words like "auger," "sump pump," "neckbones," and "uptown." I attended bingos, fundraisers, ice fishing derbies, dog-sled races, powwows, rodeos, and a deluge of sporting events. While I found these exciting, new, and adventurous, I was also struck by how awkward and out of my element I was. No amount of extracurricular activities could have prepared me for this.

One had to be hardy in order to thrive in Deer Lake, or you'd better figure it out fast, if you were going to survive. It didn't take me long to realize that the soft-boiled eggs didn't survive here. And while it took me much longer to adapt to this new environment, I only survived in that little town on the lake because of immigrit and because I started dating a young man who'd been born and raised there, Nate, one of the hardiest eggs in town.

I was one of only four Asians in town when I first arrived in 1996 and, since I'd just spent the last four years in a city and at a university with a large and diverse ethnic population, I had forgotten what it was like to be gawked at or asked, "What are you?" Plus, times had changed. Hadn't they?

Not on this side of the tracks just yet.

Nate and I walked into Radio Shack one day. Amused by the fact that I hadn't set foot in a Radio Shack in years, I took my time to look around. Nate went in first and exchanged greetings and dialogue with the lady behind the counter, who clearly knew him. As I passed her a little while later, I smiled at her.

She looked directly at me and said, "Following your man like a good Chinese wife."

Um, *excuuuuse me*? I was rendered speechless. I looked at her in disbelief, paused, and then spun around on one heel before storming out of there. Nate hadn't heard her comment, so when he got back to the car, he was surprised to see me so bothered, steam still billowing out of my ears. When I repeated what she had said to me, I didn't know if I was more appalled by her racism or her sexism.

Years later, after Deer Lake experienced a significant migration of Filipino foreign workers, someone assumed that I was Filipina and asked Nate, "Aren't they great? They even shine your shoes!"

"Nope, mine doesn't do that. What's the return policy?" Nate quipped.

And, while I had actually experienced far more racial microaggressions in Calgary, I was still shocked to find out some people in Deer Lake had never lived or even traveled anywhere else. And they were perfectly content with that. I couldn't help but feel like an exotic bird who had flown into a lake town full of fish.

My ethnicity wasn't the only culture gap that people pointed out about me. As per the usual, my body drew a great deal of attention in that little town, as well.

I have my mom's body. A petite, curvy, well-proportioned, well-defined, compact physique. I hadn't really paid much attention to my body, at first. It did what I asked of it without complaining. Or so I thought.

While at university, I befriended a girl who was a vegetarian, a concept I hadn't even thought about before. She told me she didn't like the way she felt after eating meat, so she'd stopped. Then, she asked me how I felt after eating meat. My mind went blank. I had never thought about how I felt after eating meat. In fact, I had never asked myself about how my body felt after anything at all.

This was a turning point for me and one that changed my relationship to my body. I started going to the gym. I took yoga and group fitness classes for the first time. I stopped eating meat, frozen food, and processed meals. I noticed new muscle definition in my arms and abs after only a couple of workouts. I went to the gym often and loved how I felt after a workout or a fitness class. My body changed from a softer, lumpier version of itself to a more svelte, defined, and stronger me. I felt secure and confident in my body, and, for the first time since I had entered womanhood, I saw my body as beautiful, powerful, and even sexy.

And since movement came easily to me and I was a natural-born teacher, teaching others to move was the next logical step. I became a certified group-fitness instructor at the age of nineteen. I learned choreography quickly, mapped a class in my mind from beginning to end, and guided my students in discovering their own bodies with pride. I had finally found a way to use my body with intention, purpose, and productivity, which contributed to others' wellbeing as well as to mine. My body went from weapon to machine.

I spent hours making mixed cassette tapes with songs rearranged at 128 or 132 beats per minute, as well as choreographing step routines, hi/low, circuit, bootcamp, kickboxing, HIIT, and Tae Bo (anyone remember that?). I pretty much lived at gyms, rec centers, schools, and studios. The moment I hooked the microphone belt onto my waist, slid on the headset, and boomed out the proverbial "test, test," I felt a sense of ownership, responsibility, and, yes, belonging.

Moreover, teaching fitness not only allowed me to relive the joy I'd felt being in my body as a little girl, I was in full expression of the purest version of myself. I could get excited and express myself in my bigness without being told to be quieter or smaller, and I didn't look for external validation, as it was already built in.

So, when I got to Deer Lake after graduating from university, the first place I went to was, of course, the gym. When I told them I was a fitness instructor, they hired me on the spot. That was the easy part; everything after that proved to be more challenging. The setup was archaic. They had old, painted, wooden steps, no microphone, and an old portable stereo system that could only be set up at the very front of a large, full-sized gymnasium, directly below the upstairs gym, where classes were small and poorly attended.

My outgoing nature took me to the streets to drum up some interest and excitement around joining the evening fitness classes that I led after teaching middle school.

Unfortunately, it wasn't met with the same enthusiasm. After hearing excuses like it wasn't at the right time or it was too exposed (in full gawking view of the runners on the treadmills upstairs), I soon realized that some women weren't coming because of... me! And, well, my body.

As a fitness instructor, I was used to putting myself "out there" for all to see, hear, and, yes, judge. However, after a class or two, we'd all come to a mutual understanding that nobody was being compared to anybody else and we were all "in it" together in the name of health and fitness. But these women had made their judgment about me long before trying my class. The women who found me and my body intimidating replied to my invitation with, "Um, are you kidding me? No way! *Look* at you! I could never keep up with your classes." Despite reassuring them it wasn't like that, I came to accept that I'd never be afforded the opportunity to share my gifts with them even one time.

My young, fit energy carried out onto the bar dance floor. I loved music and grooved naturally to Asian and African fusion beats. So, while I found it challenging to move to the guitar country twang at a bar named Truckers, dancing all night long still brought me great joy.

Although I had finally managed to honor my own self-worth, I was robbed of feeling proud of myself when some women approached me at the bar. Naïvely thinking it was a friendly gesture, I welcomed them, only to find out those same women accused me of coming to town to "steal their men."

I ran into women in the grocery store who hid the items in their cart from me, becoming all awkward and embarrassed by their food choices. Random strangers would come up to me and ask what I did for a living. When I replied "middle school teacher," they looked confused.

When I mentioned I also taught fitness classes, they nodded. "Oh, okay, yeah. *That's* why," as they waved their hands down my body.

I was at a friend's place getting ready to go out once. We were both in her bathroom, when I stepped out of the shower. Later that evening, after a few drinks, she announced to an entire crowd of people, "I saw Serena naked today. She has the *perfect* body!"

And while I get that those were all meant to be compliments in some warped way, I still struggled with the idea that, after all this time, people spent more time judging me and my intentions by the way I looked, instead of getting to know me. I had so much more to offer.

I didn't see what they saw. I didn't see comparison, and I certainly didn't see perfection. I just saw myself as a genuine, generous, and naïvely trusting young woman who, against many odds, had built enough courage to move and express herself freely and to feel at home in her own body once again.

Regardless, my immiguilt conditioning could not stand to see so many women so uncomfortable in my presence. I wanted to have the exact opposite impact on them. I wanted those women to feel motivated, alive, and lit up in my presence. Despite feeling betrayed by the feminine numerous times and in multiple ways, sisterhood is still something I deeply crave; when I feel slighted by another woman, the wound cuts deep.

So, as a young twenty-something with immiguilt, I did the only thing I knew to do at the time. I dimmed myself down, stepped out of the spotlight, shrank into second place, and made room for someone else to shine. I wore baggier clothes, I dismissed compliments about my body or my teaching style, and I even started filling my grocery cart with food that everyone else seemed to be eating.

Little did this young woman know at the time, but this would be the first of many more scrutiny tests of her "perfect body" and her relationship to perfectionism, no matter what side of the tracks she found herself on.

Chapter 8
CRAB FOR LUNCH

I HAD LIVED IN DEER LAKE for only two years before I decided to call it quits, leaving a permanent teaching contract, and Nate, behind. In 1998, I moved to a city just north of Calgary where I got another middle school teaching job, which meant Nate and I were testing out a long-distance relationship. For the next three years, we saw each other every few weeks, either meeting halfway in Edmonton or driving down south to Calgary together on weekends. We were both still in our twenties, so neither of us seemed to mind the untethered arrangement.

I was busy and liked it that way. I taught middle school during the day, coached several school athletic teams before and after school, led group fitness and yoga classes at a local gym in the evenings, and was on the road most weekends. I was a young, fit, twenty-four-year-old firecracker who said yes to life and its abundant opportunities that tended to fall into my lap.

Go on safari to Africa although I disliked camping? Yes! Get my PADI scuba diving certification even though I could barely swim? Sure! Become a certified yoga teacher, even though I hardly practiced? Why not?

I also applied this "yes" concept to teaching. Since I didn't have pets, partners, or prodigy, I often ended up being the teacher who said "yes" to coaching teams, supervising events, going on school trips, and driving the seventy-two-passenger school bus wherever and whenever it was needed.

While I certainly thrived by learning, creating, and contributing in this way, I was also completely unaware of my limitations. Feeling limitless in my twenties, I never seemed to notice that my plate was too full until it was too late. I often said "yes" for the sake of pleasing and so as not to disappoint others, but also because I knew I could do the job. And since everyone has limits, saying "yes" resulted in a slow-burning fireball of overwhelm and resentment developing in the pit of my stomach.

To make matters worse, I was completely oblivious to that slow burn or to how my lack of boundaries affected others. In my naïve mind, I thought, by doing more, I was doing others a favor. I had been teaching for six years, and the reality was I didn't have much left at the end of the day. Also, whether I'd admit it or not, my relationships were suffering. The people I was closest to could feel the searing heat of my imminent burnout a mile away. Especially my students.

One day, I was leaning up against the edge of the lecture podium at the front of my classroom. It was last period, and my Grade 7 late French-immersion students were working diligently to finish up their science lab reports, so they could avoid having it for homework.

As I stared out the classroom window, my mind drifted. My after-school to-do list scrolled through my head: photocopy tomorrow's quiz, drive to the gym, teach my 4:30

p.m. cardio class, grab groceries, make dinner, plan tomorrow's lesson…

These lists ruled the record album of my daily life, but lately, it felt like the needle was stuck on repeat. The same curriculum, the same four classroom walls, the same Pavlov's dog routine, where I ate, peed, and taught on a bell. "Is this it?" I would often ask myself. There's got to be more to life than working like a (Pavlov's) dog for ten months of the year and recovering for a few weeks, only to do the exact same thing all over again? Right? Would I be donning my neon-pink recess supervision sash and stomping the snow off my boots at the sound of the bell until I was old and gray?

Don't get me wrong. There are millions of incredibly dedicated teachers out there who deserve far more respect than they get. And I personally really enjoyed teaching middle school. I loved the freedom of creativity, appreciated the learning process, and actually thrived in the daily unpredictability of working with hormonal humans. But, deep down, I knew there was something more waiting for me outside of these four classroom walls. I was an exotic bird, perched upon one of four thin edges of a cardboard box I had put myself into. My longing for more wasn't going to disappear just because I changed curriculums or schools or towns.

A colleague once asked me what I wanted to do, if I wasn't teaching, and I replied, "I want to own a wellness retreat center somewhere warm." So, what happened next was a blessing in disguise, a calling that woke me up out of my complacent conditioned immigrit slumber.

"Madame Arora!" a young voice called from the middle of the room.

Snapping me out of my to-do list daydream, I scanned the room. One of the girls in class sat upright at her desk, her arm straight up in the air, staring at me confidently.

"Oui, cocotte?" I answered, returning to the present moment. Cocotte is a French slang word I used often with my students as a term of endearment, kind of like how my dad calls me "beta" in Hindi.

"Madame, did you have crab for lunch?" she asked.

A hush fell over the room and all eyes turned to me. Whenever my students spoke to me in English, we knew it was serious.

I looked at her, confused. *Huh*? I thought to myself, trying to make sense of her question.

Quickly checking the front of my shirt, swiping the side of my face, even smelling my breath, I replied, "No. Why?"

Without missing a beat, this young girl, who was known to speak her mind, sat up taller and declared, "Because you're *crabby!*" Then, she nonchalantly put her pencil back down and continued her work.

Partially amused, partially stunned, I didn't know what to make of her witty accusation. The other kids sat motionless, holding their breath as they awaited my response.

Dang, I thought to myself. *Is it* that *obvious*? Gah! Of course it was. If there was one thing I knew, kids read energy better than they do textbooks. I cracked a weak smile that broadened across my entire face, apologized, and thanked her for her honesty. The other kids exhaled and giggled under their grins.

It was a lightbulb moment for me. My students deserved the best version of me, and their success was directly dependent on my level of commitment to them.

And while I felt like I was a good teacher and had contributed the best I knew how, I didn't quite realize the effect I would have on these young souls for years to come.

Plus, I had promised myself from day one, I would never be one of "those" teachers. You know, the teachers who are buying time, hoping their pension reaches its limit before they do. Had I already reached my limit after only six years? Was my time in the classroom up? One thing was certain. I couldn't keep waiting around to find out. Because doing that would impact too many people, and not for the better. And those kids certainly deserved more.

So, once again, I said "yes" to life and acted quickly, applying for a leave of absence for the following school year, in 2001.

A few months later, I spread my wings and took a leap of faith, trusting that whatever was waiting for me outside of those four classroom walls or that cardboard box didn't serve crab for lunch.

SERENA ARORA

Chapter 9
ASIA, AUZ, AND CANCER

IN 2001, WITH MY LEAVE OF absence imminent, Nate also applied to do a teacher exchange in Australia, with the idea we would meet up there in six months. My plan was to travel to Southeast Asia first. So, instead of setting up my classroom and attending staff meetings that following fall, I was elbowing my way through the busy bus station in Chiang Mai, Thailand. The air was a thick mixture of bus exhaust, sweet-smelling BBQ food stalls, and sweaty humans. The bus I was to catch that day was a bumpy, winding, uphill ride three hours north to the little riverside town of Pai.

I arrived at the Chiang Mai bus station early, so I could get to Pai before dark. I was waiting in line when the bus pulled up to the station. The locals immediately jostled me, pushing past me to board the bus. Lineups and lanes don't really mean too much in Asian countries like these, especially when it comes to transportation. If you need to be somewhere, it is every human, dog, and cow for themselves.

I finally managed to squeeze into the back of the bus before the doors closed. After scanning all the rows, I claimed a small space on the very back bench of the bus, beside a small Thai man. Reluctantly, he made space for me instead of his large rice sacks, rearranging them on the floor before gesturing for me to sit down. I acknowledged his invitation then sat down on the bench beside him, my knees up by my elbows and a mountain of rice sacks beneath my feet. I felt the sharp corner of a metal cage press into my thigh as it slid from his lap onto mine. Inside, two live chickens flapped about.

To my right, an elderly silver-haired Thai woman kept clearing her throat loudly. She dug through her bag and pulled out some kind of essential oil or smelling salts then proceeded to stuff up each nostril, followed by a loud sniff. Beside her sat a young Thai lady, tightly clutching two grocery bags under one arm and her toddler in the other. Snot ran down the little boy's nose onto his upper lip then was lapped up by his tiny pink tongue. He looked up at me with his watery saucer-like eyes and blinked slowly with the patience and wisdom of an old man, as though he had taken this three-hour journey on his mom's lap a million times in his short life.

With rice sacks under my feet, a chicken cage on half my lap, bodily fluids from the snot-nosed kid on the other half, and wafts of Asian oils and armpits, I sat back, closed my eyes, and smiled. It was my twenty-seventh birthday, and, completely in my element, I couldn't think of a better way to celebrate it. Like my mom, I found traveling exhilarating. It breathed life into my very being and instilled a level of freedom and gratitude unlike anything else in my life ever could. It was the best birthday gift ever—thanks, cocotte!

After four months of travel through Southeast Asia, I left behind the various tuk-tuks, temples, Thai massage training, and Thai cooking lessons I had been exploring and went on to immerse myself in family, food, and yoga training in India.

When my yogi uncle asked me why I had come to India to study yoga, I replied, "Because, Uncle, I wanted to study yoga from the source."

He replied, "My dear beta, you don't study yoga. You *are* yoga." His profound response was both encouraging and shaming in a way only a senior Arora family member can do. "Now, go back home, and become a dentist or information technology professional," he concluded.

This was my first visit as an adult, having traveled to India for the first time at only four years old. As a kid in this environment, I remember soaking up the abundant hugs, kisses, and familial love that came from our large extended family on my dad's side. As a North American adult who was no longer accustomed to being hugged and loved up, I wasn't expecting to be welcomed in the same loving and affectionate manner. I couldn't have been more wrong. The unbreakable blood bond is an integral part of our family, and I gratefully received their unconditional love.

Being an Arora in India was interesting. "Arora" in India is the North American equivalent to "Smith" or "Johnson," so if you're an Arora, you're historically Indian. With that, you would think I'd feel at home in India, with an immediate sense of belonging; however, just as I had felt in Chinese school with the Chinese kids, I was also unlike the Indians in India. I hadn't grown up there, didn't speak the language, and because I didn't fully "look the part," I felt compelled to prove my Indian-ness to complete strangers.

Tourists are often taken advantage of, charged more by rickshaw drivers and food vendors, so my uncle told me to put my sunglasses on when we hailed a taxi, in order to "hide my Chinese eyes." I had to argue with a security guard because he didn't believe I was of Indian descent, finally flashing my passport in his face and saying emphatically in my very North American accent, "See! I'm an Arora! *ARORA!*"

Despite this passport flashing, the guard still wasn't convinced. I felt more dejected at being dismissed by this random security guard in New Delhi than I had by Alan, the kid in the back of the school bus who'd indirectly called me "Paki" when I was twelve.

I experienced culture gaps everywhere I went. Even in my country of origin. Feeling rejected when I'm in a sea of white is one thing, but being rejected by another brown face is felt in my bones. It hurts in a way I can't explain, far beyond that of a microaggression or racial slur. Being rejected by your own people is the ultimate betrayal.

Maybe my disappointment felt so severe because I had such high hopes I would find belonging in India and that it would feel like home to me. In the end, my yogi uncle was right. Whether through my family name or the practice of yoga, I would never find belonging by searching for it outside of myself. It had to come from within.

He planted a seed in my heart that would root and grow over time. I would eventually understand what he meant by *being* yoga. For now, however, I was heading Down Under.

Over the next six months, I travelled first to Australia, where I met Nate and my mom's eldest sister. Then, I went to New Zealand, where I connected with the spirits of my deceased friend and late Chinese grandfather while I hiked fifteen miles in four hours. Next, to Singapore, the cleanest city in the world, where I happened to snag the last hostel bed, which came with bed bugs. And to Malaysia, where I did end up eating crab—the best crab I've ever eaten, by the way—before heading home to Calgary after ten months of globetrotting to surprise my mom on her birthday in 2002.

After surprising my family at my mom's birthday dinner, I spent the evening with my immediate family, answering questions, recapping parts of my trip, and providing updates on our relatives overseas.

Afterward, when my mom and I were alone at the kitchen table, she asked me, "Did you notice anything about my hair?"

Since hair changes day to day in my world and I hadn't seen my mom for almost a year, I answered, "Well, it's a little straighter, I guess."

"It's a wig," she said.

Scrutinizing her black locks a little closer, I furrowed my brow and said, "Why are you wearing a wig?"

"Because I have cancer," she replied.

I stared back at her. The color seemed to drain out of the room as though a sepia filter washed over my lens.

"Cancer?" I whispered.

She started to tell me about her lumpectomy, chemotherapy, and upcoming radiation treatments as though she was checking off a grocery list. My eyes dropped to the table as I furiously wrung my hands, and then a wave of tears burst from me like a broken dam. Finally, it registered. Some family members whom I met during my trip had kept asking me, "How's your mom?" "Have you talked to your mom yet?" I hadn't connected the dots, but now it was clear. My family hadn't wanted to tell me in fear I would cut my trip short and come home earlier than I did.

As mentioned, I'm a "jump into action" girl, especially when it comes to crises and emergencies. So, for this particular crisis, the jump was into what I did best. Educate myself so I could "fix" it.

I delved into yoga therapy, Ayurveda, and got my master's degree in holistic therapy. I quit my teaching job, moved into my parents' basement, taught yoga and fitness full time in Calgary, and led yoga teacher trainings at nearby retreats.

My ambition for supporting my mom's healing and recovery after her cancer treatment was to systematically implement all the new natural-medicine practices I had learned. My mom didn't believe in holistic medicine, but in conjunction with her radiation treatment, she trusted me enough to change her diet, household products, and even her perspective on natural self-care remedies, which she has maintained to this very day.

It worked. Two years later, in 2004, my cancer-free mom and I were walking in the park beside their house. I asked her what she was thinking about. She said, "Oh, I was just thinking about how lucky I am to be healthy and walking every day... Because of you."

Hmm, I thought to myself. I might have been the one to learn the talk, but my mom had enough courage to walk it. My mom's recovery was the first way in which I nurtured the seed within, proving my yogi uncle right: one can learn as many modalities and techniques as you want, but it's only when you *embody* those practices consistently that, over time, they become the wisdom that heals.

SERENA ARORA

I literally traveled to the other side of the world seeking answers, only to come back home a year later and fully commit to embodied healing. I had found my calling.

But something else was calling first—Nate.

Chapter 10
GOD, GIVE ME A SIGN

AT THE END OF 2004, the night before Christmas Eve, the Alberta winter highways were busy with cars and trucks heading to wherever they needed to be for the holidays. As it does in places that far north of the equator, the sun was beginning to set, even though it was only 4:00 p.m.

The road-conditions app showed yellow and red lines, indicating drifting snow and icy patches on the stretches of highway to the north. *Well,* I thought to myself, *if anything does happen, I have everything I need.* My entire life was packed into my car like a Tetris game. I had moved a lot over the last few years, so I had gotten really good at packing my green Honda CRV, Jade (pronounced j-aw-d, thanks to a feisty little grade-one French student of mine who emphatically corrected me on the pronunciation of her name). I knew exactly which items, depending on their shape, weight, and flexibility, fit into every nook and cranny of that SUV, from the floor to the ceiling.

Since coming back from my Australasia trip, I had been teaching yoga and fitness classes and leading yoga teacher trainings and healthy-living retreats full time in Calgary for two years. During that time, Nate had come back from

Australia and returned to his old teaching position in Deer Lake.

After many conversations, Nate and I decided to take our relationship off the backburner. We had sustained a long-distance relationship for eight years, including being on opposite sides of the world for nearly a year. While I had convinced myself this was a healthy dynamic for two people in their late twenties—an ebbing and flowing helix of individuation and connection through life—now that I was thirty, it was time for me to make a responsible adult decision.

The decision was made. I would move back to Deer Lake and open up a group home for troubled youth with Nate.

I had been driving north for three hours and was passing the halfway point, an industrial suburb on the outskirts of Edmonton. It was the last real chance for convenience and "civilization," as I called it—a decent bathroom, gas, good food options, and a Starbucks. For me, the halfway point on this drive also often brought a wave of emotions with it.

Perhaps this sounds ridiculous to some, but I always felt a sense of relief, security and safety whenever I was driving south, toward the green Starbucks sign, knowing whatever I needed or wanted would be at my fingertips and emergency rescue was only seconds away. On the other hand, whenever I was driving north, it felt as though my safety blanket (and cell phone coverage) was slowly slipping through my fingers as I watched the Starbucks sign recede in the rearview mirror.

Intermittent static started to cut into the music I was listening to on the radio. As I searched for a clearer channel,

I heard blips of music, cut-off voices, and long periods of crackling until my car speakers buzzed into the sound of pure oblivion, *tssshhhhhhhhhhh.*

And then it hit me. Had I really thought this through? Was I, too, fading off into oblivion as I continued to drive north? Did I really want to move back to that little town on the lake? Would it be any different this time around? I knew nothing about opening a group home for youth... What was I thinking? I was so content and at the peak of my health, living in Calgary. Couldn't Nate and I continue the way we had been for the last eight years...? Was moving back really worth it?

My eyes started to well up. Then, I did something I had never done before. I called out to God. Shouting over the static, I exclaimed, "God! I know I don't talk to you very often, or at all really, but I need your help right now. Just tell me what to do. Do I keep going? Or do I turn around? I can turn around right now. It's not too late. I'm only halfway. Tell me, God, is this a mistake? I need a sign, God! GIVE ME A SIGN!"

The sky was getting dark and tears blurred my vision, so I hadn't seen the truck tailing me until a bright flash of light blinded me in the rearview mirror. Just then, the lights swerved off to the right, and a big black pickup truck sped up beside me on the passenger side. Annoyed that I'd been driving in the fast lane and hadn't been paying attention to my dwindling speed, the angry driver swerved his truck back into my lane, cutting me off, and kicking up a blinding white snowstorm with his tires.

I slowed down to this proverbial middle finger that drivers did in order to say, "Learn to drive, you effing moron, or get outta the fast lane!"

As the snow subsided, my headlights shone on the bumper of his truck. I could barely make out a sticker on its bumper. And, just like that, like angels singing through the radio static, God's sign appeared in front of me. The bumper sticker read, *It's alright to be a redneck.*

I blinked a few times, read it again, and, with my resistant immigrit, started to reason out loud with God. "Soooo, what are you saying? I keep going? Which way are the rednecks?"

Alone with my thoughts, I kept driving, past the last-chance gas station and into the dark. I reflected on how great my life had been over the last few years. My mom was in full remission, I loved my career as a fitness and yoga teacher trainer, and I was in the best shape of my life.

According to North American standards, I was the epitome of health. My body was ripped, flexible, and agile, plus, I could stand on my head, balance on my hands, and pistol squat for days. I ate quinoa and spirulina for breakfast, large serving-bowl size organic salads for lunch, kale, root vegetables, and brown rice for dinner, and I drank almond golden milk before bed. I lived in gyms, studios… and my car.

Yes, as a full-time yoga and fitness instructor in Calgary, my days were spent driving to different locations across the city, teaching no less than five yoga and fitness classes per day every day of the week. In those days, there was more demand for yoga classes than there were actual studios available, so I'd teach at gyms, rec centers, schools, YMCAs, private homes, and even on conference tables in office boardrooms. I'd lug a giant hockey bag full of props, bands, disks, blocks, belts, and yoga mats with me. Moreover, Calgary is a big, sprawling city, so leaving enough room between classes to get to the next place on time was no small feat.

One day, my calculations were off, and I was running behind to get to my second yoga class of the morning at another gym across the city. After cursing the string of red lights and significant traffic for a Tuesday morning, I also ended up having to wait for a long, old-school freight train to pass! Of course. While all the other drivers waited patiently in their cars beside me, I was pretty sure they could hear the muffled, drawn-out sounds coming from inside my car. "Fuuuuuuuuck! I'm laaaaaate!"

When I finally made it to the gym with one minute to spare, I bolted past the front desk, slammed my giant hockey bag on the ground, shoved a cassette in the tape deck, flipped my yoga mat out with a crack, sat down, closed my eyes, and let out an exasperated, "And breathe…"

The irony was astonishing.

I had focused so much on teaching yoga that I had stopped *being* it. I could feel my yogi uncle's disappointed head bobble all the way from India.

The truth was I had unwittingly used teaching to avoid feeling emotions that made me uncomfortable, sad, or scared. I felt great when I worked out and taught classes, so the obvious answer seemed clear to me. Do more of that. To stay and teach within my comfort zone. But the Universe had a different idea.

On the outside, I was as healthy as they come. What you couldn't see, though, was my excessive worry built from fear or my "more is better" mentality built from shame, and my easily annoyed short temper built from guilt. Especially with my parents—immiguilt.

I hadn't lived with my parents since I was seventeen, so the standard surveillance, unsolicited advice, and direct judgments about what, when, and how I should do things felt significantly more irritating to me at thirty.

You see, the parent-child relationship in Eastern culture doesn't automatically change like it does in Western culture. In the West, parents consider their kids adults when they turn a certain age, and they shift into a peer relationship of equality and even friendship. This important milestone is when Western parents expect their kids to develop agency, take accountability over their own actions, assume adult responsibilities like making their own money, budgeting living expenses, and leaving their childhood home to manage their own.

In contrast, Eastern parents consider themselves authority figures over their children and, no matter how old their kids are, demand a certain level of respect and subordination from them. Eastern parents don't think of their kids as anything else but kids, and they treat them as such because it's worked for them. And when you're treated like a kid, it's much easier to fall into the role of acting like one and adopting kid-like behaviors, reactions, and responsibilities (or lack thereof), even as an adult. So, adult children of Eastern descent often stay at home well into early adulthood. This dynamic leaves very little room for parental emancipation at any age.

Asian parents in particular would never consider themselves peers to their adult children, let alone friends. And herein lies the conflict between Asian immigrant parents and their adult children, who are, for all intents and purposes, Western. And as much as these adult children yearn to have peer-adult relationships with their immigrant parents, the culture gap doesn't allow for it.

In my forties, I was once complaining to a friend about how my parents still treat me like a kid, when her husband piped up and said, "Well, stop acting like one then."

I took it to heart and decided to consciously and deliberately redefine my adult relationship with my parents.

It has proven to be an uphill battle. When I was forty-eight, after stating a fact to my mom, she blurted out, "Oh, come off it. You're just a kid!"

When I was forty-nine, my dad still told me what lane to drive in and where I should park, as though I were a fifteen-year-old new driver with a learner's license. Didn't my dad know that, as a gym teacher, I drove a seventy-two-passenger school bus?

And that's just it. I found it disappointing, how incurious they were about what I had accomplished in my life, how much I'd done, and how broadly I'd lived. And if I showed any kind of savviness, my dad was surprised. He'd say, "How do you know that?"

I found it disheartening to know how little my parents acknowledged me and my accomplishments. And patronizing, given that, though I'm almost fifty, they still called me "a kid."

One thing I've observed, though, is that they don't treat my older sister who has children this way. So, I've come up with a theory.

While Western parents consider age a rite of passage into adulthood, I believe that first-generation immigrant parents don't think of their adult children *as* adults until they have had children of their own. I mean, let's face it, it's difficult to call your kid "a kid" when another kid is calling them "Mom," right? So, according to my theory, I will never pass my parents' threshold of adulthood in this lifetime. Without ever having kids of my own, perhaps I've forfeited the ability to change the traditional Asian power dynamic between my immigrant parents and myself.

Moreover, living with my parents as an adult afforded me the opportunity to observe their marriage dynamic, too. The tough love that they showed us as kids was amplified tenfold in their own marriage. Criticism, scolding, and badgering were their forms of communication, and full-on shouting matches would break out once one of them was pushed to their limit. This was the definition of love and marriage modeled for me from a young age, and since my parents had been married for thirty-four years at that point, something about it seemed unconditional.

Which brings me to my own romantic partnership. There I was at thirty, in a very long, long distance relationship that no longer felt ideal. And while living with my parents at thirty wasn't healthy for me, the thought of moving back to Deer Lake didn't feel great, either. However, the prospect of living with Nate again, starting a new business, and teaching yoga somewhere new not only felt comfortable to me, but also like a good adult decision at the time.

So, I sighed out loud, gripped the steering wheel, pressed down hard on the gas pedal, and headed north to Deer Lake for the second time, this time taking all my adult baggage with me.

Chapter 11

GOODBYE, SERENA

I STOOD AT THE PEDESTRIAN crossing of the main intersection of Deer Lake. It was January 2005, and the chilly air was thick with the after-holiday lull. People grabbed at woolen scarves on their necks, pulling them up higher onto their faces, as they darted in and out of the warm buildings leading to the main intersection of town.

The minimal variety in store options available in this little town left a bad taste on my spoiled, city-slicker palate, but I doubled down on my immigrit and pushed on, hopping from one Dollar Store to the next. Old-school Christmas lights and gaudy tinsel-decorated lamp posts twinkled in the sunlight in the shapes of gift boxes, bells, and mistletoe. An elderly lady swept snow off the front porch of her candy shop, and a group of young teenagers gathered across the street, impatiently jabbing at the pedestrian-crossing button as though playing a Whac-A-Mole game.

I shivered as I waited, a stark reminder I wasn't in Kansas anymore, Toto, or in Calgary for that matter. After I had spent the Christmas holidays with Nate and his family at their family farm, he had gone back to his full-time teaching job, and my new adventure, Operation Group Home, was in full swing.

Owning and running a group home for troubled youth wasn't even close to being on my radar, and it was a far cry from anything I remotely knew or could have even imagined doing. Nate, on the other hand, had a sound understanding of this world and his role in it. So, while opening a group home was his idea, this new business venture fulfilled a value of mine, as well: comfort. I believe every kid deserves a safe, comfortable home to grow up in. And because I experienced this growing up, my new project felt personal and strangely optimistic at the time.

While I was intrigued by the prospect of providing a comfortable home for these kids, I had limited experience serving an underprivileged population, especially in this way. I was about to learn the hard way that comfortable meant something very different to the naïve, pre-group-home me than it did to those kids, their families, and their social workers.

When the light turned green, I stepped into the street, expecting the impatient kids on the other side to start running toward me. But they didn't budge. They didn't even walk. They stood on the street corner, frozen, huddled together like statues and they gawked at me making my way across. And they weren't the only ones staring. Drivers on either side of the road sat in their cars, eyes fixed on me and following my every step with their heads. Even the old woman on the candy store porch stopped sweeping and stared at me as I crossed the road.

Hm, I thought. *That's strange.* I glanced down at the front of my pants then quickly checked my backside. Nothing seemed out of the ordinary to me. The frosty air made it easy to shrug it off, so I quickened my pace, found my car, jumped into the frozen seat, and drove back to Nate's little acreage home by the lake just outside of town.

When I got there, I swung the door open, clumsily stumbled inside, and stomped the snow off my knee-high Fluevog boots. As I dropped a flock of shopping bags onto the floor in a haphazard pile, I noticed the fire in the wood-burning stove was fading. I instinctively swung the stove door open and tossed in another log as though I had done it a thousand times.

Squinting at the flying ash, I blew gently until I was convinced the new log had caught the flame before slamming the stove door shut. As I wiped a dusting of ash from my forehead, I caught a glimpse of my reflection in the full-length mirror. And suddenly, everything came to a halt.

There I was, in my striped, flared-sleeved sweater, vintage velour cords, red knee-high, button-down boots, and bright-purple fringe lining my edgy, asymmetrical haircut. As I stared into the mirror, I slid a purple bang off my face and tucked it behind my ear. And then, it dawned on me. All those people at the crosswalk today did indeed see something out of the ordinary. *Me.* They were staring at me because, well, I stuck out in that little town like the proverbial sore thumb.

I was so familiar with the unchanged aesthetics of this town, it didn't occur to me that my own had changed dramatically while I was away. My fashion sense was also a little out of the ordinary, I'll admit. I didn't follow trends, bought and wore what I liked, and for years not only had I never doubted my look, I often received compliments from random strangers in the city, asking who cut my hair or where I had bought my clothes.

After I had literally stopped traffic in the middle of Deer Lake, it was becoming abundantly clear to me that "out of the ordinary" wasn't exactly welcomed here.

And then, as though I was seeing my surroundings for the first time, I finally saw what everyone else saw. My gaze went from the parquet flooring in Nate's cabin home to the dial-up Internet I couldn't believe still existed, to the old-school forest-green backsplash in the kitchen, and then to my red-and-purple, high-class-hippie reflection in the mirror. It felt like I was watching that *Sesame Street* segment, "One of these things is not like the other."

As my reflection stared back at me knowingly, my vision blurred in the heat coming off the wood stove. After refocusing my eyes, it was still blurry, but this time from my own tears.

It was true: one of these things was definitely not like the others, and one of them certainly didn't belong. There I was again, firmly planted in the culture gap between myself and this small town—the same little town I had decided to leave eight years before. Though I had already lived there, I was no longer the same person.

Over the past eight years, I had quit teaching, traveled across four continents, become a yoga therapist and teacher trainer, earned a master's degree in holistic medicine, and was now in my thirties. I had changed—but this town hadn't.

The slow realization began to sink in: I was going to be too much for this little town.

So, in typical comfort-restoring patterning, I did what was familiar. I dug deep into the immigrit pit of my stomach and pulled out the strength I needed to move forward. I had made the decision to move back to Deer Lake for the second time, so I buried any emotions that might deter me or make me question my choice. I was determined not to fail at this. Not again. This was the heart of immigrit.

So, I looked in the mirror straight into my slanted "shit-brown" eyes, swallowed hard, and muttered out loud, "Goodbye, Serena."

I unzipped my flared sleeve sweater, slid it off, and placed it in the very back of a drawer, where it wouldn't see the light of day in that little town again. Then, I grabbed the Dollar Store bags, plunked them on the table, and got back to work.

Saying goodbye to that version of me was yet another example of how I had learned to dim my expression in order to create comfort for others. And little did I know, running a group home was going to test my own comfort level a hundredfold.

I had lived a privileged life, littered with opportunities that kept me busy and far away from the life these kids were born into. These kids were born into family situations that social services had deemed unfit or dangerous to their wellbeing, which meant they had been removed from their home and placed in group homes like ours. Not only were group homes immeasurably out of my comfort zone, I'd had no idea they even existed. I was blind and naïve to this part of society, so not only did I struggle to relate to the kids, but most of my days left me in disbelief, discouraged, and even depressed. Each week, I read intake forms that sounded like horror movie scripts: addiction, abandonment, abuse, stabbings, shootings, and suicide—words used far too often for my sheltered ears. But for these kids, it was all they knew.

This life was so far from my field of consciousness that, once I realized what I had gotten myself into, I felt like a Disney princess making her way through the big, bad, dark world of violence, physical restraints, court orders, and jail. Let's just say this was one Disney movie that did not end well for the princess.

And while group home work is unpredictable, extremely challenging, and 24/7, I still somehow believed we could be the ones to "rescue" these kids from the underbelly of humanity. On the contrary, I was grossly unprepared and unskilled for this job. I found myself unclogging toilets, straddling bathtubs full of sewer water, restraining and deescalating kids taller and at least ten to twenty pounds heavier than me, and getting woken up in the middle of the night because a kid went AWOL (absent without leave), and we had to go look for them. I was called a "fucking cunt" more times in one week than I had heard those words strung together in my entire life. I'd get called a "black-ass bitch" (apparently referring to my excessive lordotic curve and round butt) in the morning and then, in the afternoon, sit across from former teaching colleagues, social workers, judges, and police officers, advocating for that same name-calling kid.

I not only ended up in another culture chasm, I literally found myself in a leaky lifeboat, knee-deep up shit creek, holding nothing but a toilet plunger. And yet, however ill-equipped and over my head I was, I, of course, refused to fail and soldiered on—immigrit.

At 5:00 a.m. one chilly fall morning, I had to drive one of the new group-home girls to her court appearance in her hometown, a four-hour drive away. The girl was fourteen, quiet and sweet, though she didn't say much. We climbed into my SUV, Jade, and headed out into the sunrise.

I kept the conversation going while she listened intently—or so it seemed. I joked about how the sunrise reflected against Jade's sideview mirrors, making a shadow on the road shaped like Shrek. I laughed. She didn't. I asked her open-ended questions, but I was lucky if I got a one-word answer. More often, it was just silence. With hit-and-miss radio stations and CDs that, to a fourteen-year-old, probably sounded like Frank Sinatra or Nina Simone, it was one of the longest four-hour road trips of my life.

When we arrived, we waited for her social worker to show up. She didn't. After leaving several messages with no response, I quickly realized I would have to help this young girl navigate the court hearing by myself. I had never been inside a courthouse until I opened the group home. And, even then, this was only my second court hearing with a group-home kid. Since this girl was new to us, I didn't know how many times she'd been to court in her fourteen short years or even what had landed her there. I was going in blind.

What I did learn in that small-town courthouse, however, was that this girl's mother was quite famous in town. And by "famous," I mean she was well-known by the police, peace officers, remand centers, courthouse staff, lawyers, and other local law enforcement. So, sadly, they weren't surprised to see her daughter following in her footsteps.

The court was called to order, and her case was announced. It was her turn. Her social worker still hadn't arrived. The court-appointed counsel spoke on her behalf, but as civil hearings for minors often go, without the social worker and not enough evidence to proceed, the judge decided to postpone the hearing. Postpone her hearing? We had just driven four hours for nothing? And I'd have to come back and do it all over again in a few months?

I stood up to leave. The court attorney waved me down and told me the young girl had been taken next door to the police station for fingerprints and would meet me there.

I was standing just inside the doors of the police station when a disheveled woman in her late thirties rushed in. She glanced at me and introduced herself, last name first. It was the girl's social worker. She quickly explained how she had forgotten about the hearing, apologized briefly, and then asked where the girl was, so she could meet her.

Meet her? She hadn't even met her yet? I told her the girl was in the back, getting her fingerprints taken, and we'd be heading back to the group home after that.

The social worker and I made small talk while we waited for what seemed like an eternity. Finally, a police officer came out. He must have known the social worker, because he motioned for both of us to follow him to the back of the station and opened the door without a word.

When we entered the small room, I saw the girl. Another officer was holding a pen in one hand and the girl's wrist in the other.

When he saw us, he informed us the girl had finally given her fingerprints but was refusing to sign the document. He couldn't let her go without her signature.

I took that as my cue to step in. I encouraged the girl to "just sign the document," so we could get back on the road. Stoic, she stood there, her hand balled into a fist in the officer's grip.

Suddenly, she started squirming, growing more agitated. She twisted under the officer's hold, so he dropped the pen and grabbed her wrist with both hands. Then, with a quick motion, he pulled a thin, shiny object from under her sleeve. A sharp knife gleamed under the fluorescent lights.

"Ah," he said, "okay, this makes more sense now." He held up the knife and asked, "Where did you get this?"

She glanced at me. It was the small, sharp kitchen knife from the group home. Our protocol was to lock up all sharps every night and only put them back out in the morning before breakfast. Somehow, this one had gone unaccounted for.

"Did you have that with you the entire time?" I asked, dumbfounded. She nodded. "What were you going to do with it? Hurt me? Kill me?" I probed, half in jest.

Suddenly, her entire face shifted from innocent Jekyll to a demonic Hyde, her eyes bulging as she bared her teeth, turned, and leapt toward me, growling, "Yuuuuuppp!"

I just stood there, frozen. Stunned.

"That's all I needed to hear," said the officer, as he quickly spun her around, handcuffed her, and held her firmly, "She'll be spending the night in cells." He then turned to her social worker and said, "You can decide how to proceed in the morning. We're done here for now."

I walked out of the police station feeling naïve and numb. I got into my car and called the group home to let them know I was leaving the girl here and to fill out her discharge papers. Once again, it was just me, Jade, and my wave of emotions on the long drive back north to Deer Lake. I considered myself a smart, savvy, resourceful woman who had traveled the world. But this? This was next-level shit, and I was way out of my league. That day could have ended far worse than it had for me and maybe others, and I wasn't willing to wait until it did.

Nate and I decided it would be best for me to take a step back from the frontlines of the group home and work on the backend of the business, instead. We made some changes — Nate left his teaching job to work full time at the group home, while I went back to doing what I was good at: yoga. But first, I had to heal.

Our home became my sanctuary. And in true exotic-bird fashion, I proceeded to nest. Hard. We had moved out of Nate's little cabin and bought a bright bungalow just outside of town, on twenty-five acres on the lake. I picked out furniture and paint that made me feel good, added gym equipment and an infrared sauna, and splurged on handmade-glass backsplash tiles and stained-concrete kitchen countertops.

More important, I took the time to recalibrate, recover, and recharge. I hiked the dense forest trails and kayaked the lake, paddling past gray herons, bald eagles, and osprey. I watched synchronized flocks of pelicans glide over the water like stealth bombers, and spiders spinning their intricate webs, waiting patiently for unsuspecting prey to get caught in the silky ropes before furiously spinning them to their demise. I stumbled upon porcupines, beavers, and lynx. Deer, moose, and bears were regular visitors, brazenly devouring the contents of my garden, bird feeder, and compost.

As a city girl who had grown up under a neon-lit sky, I was mesmerized by nature's brilliance. I was awestruck by the constellations, the phases of the moon, and the iconic Northern Lights. After slowing my fast-paced city life, settling into small-town living, and finally feeling fully resourced, I knew it was time to share my creative gifts with others, along with this magical space—so they, too, could be held and healed by the natural world.

I revamped a small outbuilding into a private infrared sauna spa, transformed the wood stove and walkout basement into a hot yoga studio, and put an ad in the newspaper (yes, the newspaper) announcing "yoga classes." My phone rang off the hook. This was the first of many newspaper ads, articles, and business features to come.

What started with me building a fire in the wood stove and serving hot herbal tea after two classes, four evenings a week, slowly evolved over the next eight years into teaching forty classes a week, hosting wellness workshops, spa days, and donation classes every weekend for months on end. As my offerings grew, I had an entire yoga studio built from the ground up. I sourced local artisans, healers, and guest teachers to share their gifts with our community.

I directed and led therapeutic-yoga teacher trainings and spearheaded a grassroots environmental initiative, holding meetings, documentary screenings, and radio interviews. Being the only yoga teacher within a 100-mile radius, I offered classes at my studio, schools, colleges, senior centers, rec facilities, gyms, government buildings, auditoriums, community centers, banks, and even the group home. My days were long, my plate was full, and I was running full steam ahead—immigrit.

Young, fit, and vibrant, I was living my creative entrepreneurial dream. I felt dynamic, passionate, and alive... until I didn't. Saying I was deeply incongruent was an understatement. With so much criticism, judgment, and unsolicited advice, growing up, I had been robbed of the opportunity to trust my intuition and my own feelings. My self-doubt was so pervasive when I was young, I learned to trust others instead of myself. As a result, I had become a serious people-pleaser with thin skin and watery boundaries.

So, I spent my days teaching others about wellness but not embodying it myself. I rearranged my class schedule to suit others, and I chatted with students long after class was over, giving my time and energy away to others instead of keeping it for myself or Nate. I encouraged others to be mindful, but I was completely careless about my own decisions. I helped others repair the damage from making out-of-body decisions, while I burned my own candle at both ends. I promoted health and fitness but ate at irregular times, and I drank far too much alcohol for my own good.

I said "yes" to everyone and everything else, which meant I said "no" to myself almost every single day. I ignored my intuition, the red flags, and the hard conversations. Once again, despite there being less traffic here, I was *doing* yoga instead of *being* it.

My life seemingly looked great from the outside, but on the inside, I was in a constant tug of war with myself. I still wasn't sure how I felt about living in Deer Lake again or even about my relationship with Nate. We were physically back together, but we were both so busy, we barely saw each other. I had left the city lights and traffic behind, but in true immigrit fashion, my "Do more, feel less" precept had in fact tightened its grip.

Spending so much time living for others through my body cost me the chance to listen to it. My own heart had been ignored so many times, it stopped talking. So, I made decisions with my head, instead—a dangerous place to be. Winona lived up there.

When I said goodbye to the young, purple-haired Serena who'd walked across the street to the beat of her own drum in her Fluevog boots, Winona had taken her place. Not only was Winona happy to be back in the driver's seat, this time she had been drinking and getting behind the wheel.

I was incongruent in many ways, but so determined to "make it work," I chose to ignore the signs that popped up along the way every so often. One such sign was a particularly mischievous squirrel that I caught gnawing at my screen doors almost every day for months. It would bite through heavy-duty plastic coolers on the back deck, steal (only one) of my flip-flops off the front porch, and even hijacked my car one time.

I was packing things into the back of my new, black Acura RDX, which I had, of course, named "Black-Ass Bitch" (Babs for short), when I opened the driver's side door to get in. The squirrel jumped from the floor to the dash and hissed at me, as though somehow, I was the intruder, scaring the crap out of me.

Another time, I was in the basement when I heard a crash from upstairs. Nate wasn't home, so I cautiously walked upstairs to see that the back door was slightly open. I noticed a collapsed wine holder next to a bowl of apples on the table. Then, there he was! That pesky squirrel leapt across the deck and made a B-line straight across the yard, holding a green apple larger than its head in its mouth. That squirrel was my sign—my animal spirit guide.

Ah, spirit animals. It's said that one's behavior often mirrors that of their spirit animal, so when my yoga students were asked what they thought my spirit animal would be, without hesitation, they blurted out, "Squirrel!"

My thoughts went straight to the hissing, gnawing, apple-stealing squirrel that I couldn't seem to get rid of. What was it here to tell me? "Change is coming, so store the necessary provisions you'll need for the long journey ahead."

Little did I know at the time, it was a sign I could no longer ignore.

Chapter 12

FIRST MARRIAGE PROPOSAL

IN 2008, A SMALL ADVERTISEMENT for an Ayurveda cooking class in Edmonton piqued my interest. I had first learned about Ayurveda, yoga's sister science, six years prior, during an advanced therapeutic-yoga teacher training in Jacksonville, Florida. Even though I was the only non-White student in a room of sixty-five people, this was the training where I felt the most at home.

The reason it was so comfortable for me was the only two other non-White people at the training were Dr. Narayan, the Ayurvedic doctor who had come from India to teach us Ayurveda, and his wife. Since the food at the retreat center wasn't great, Dr. Narayan's wife took over the kitchen and prepared Indian food for our group throughout the remainder of the teacher training. Lucky us! I felt right at home.

And while most of the other students complained about not being able to understand Dr. Narayan's accent, he was the first non-White teacher or professor I had ever had, and I remember thinking his lectures were the most relatable part of the day for me. Even though I had heard the word *Ayurveda* only a few times before his sessions, I seemed to understand exactly what Dr. Narayan was sharing. It was as though my body already held this innate wisdom, and he was simply there to remind me of it. That's because it did.

Growing up, my dad used food as medicine—mixing spices together if we weren't feeling well, or making us eat or drink whatever concoction he made, depending on the weather. Whenever I asked what it was, his usual response was, "I don't know, but Beji (his mom) used to give it to us, and we'd feel better. So just take it."

And, in typical dramatic kid fashion, I'd put up a fight at first, reluctantly smell it, make a disgusted face even if it smelled fine, and then finally force it down my throat, adding in an extra gag or two for good measure. And sure enough, I'd always feel better the next day. In fact, I don't ever remember even being sick as a kid.

I didn't know it at the time, but my dad was teaching us how to take charge of our own health by using food as medicine, employing long-standing, proven methods of healing to prevent disease. I certainly didn't know it had a name—Ayurveda, a 5,000-year-old system of medicine from India. Ayurveda makes profound sense to me. It speaks to my soul and resonates with me on a cellular level. That formal introduction to Ayurveda with Dr. Narayan was so impactful because, for the first time, I realized I wasn't just doing yoga—I was being yoga.

I lit up when he described food as medicine, like I had always known this but had never had the words to articulate it. It felt as though someone was finally speaking my language—a dialect I understood fluently. For the first time in my life, I had related deeply to what another human being was saying. I felt understood, and in that brief moment, I finally felt like I belonged. Immediately, I wanted more of that.

So, if I was going to continue learning, expanding, and growing as a yoga professional, I knew I needed to explore Ayurveda in more depth. And living in Deer Lake meant I'd have to keep an eye out for more of those poorly advertised Ayurveda courses and cooking classes and embrace those long trips on Death Road.

Despite the drive, I actually enjoyed going to Edmonton, mostly to get groceries and supplies for ourselves and the group home. Plus, Nate's sister lived there, and we were good friends. She was unpretentious and generous, and we never seemed to run out of things to talk, laugh, or cry about. I was planning to stay with her after the cooking class that evening, but she insisted we meet up at the fancy hotel downtown for a drink first, instead. While I found her invitation to meet for a drink a bit unusual and out of character for her, I agreed.

After the cooking class, I paused just long enough to realize how grounded I felt. My body felt anchored, and my mind was at ease. In fact, for the first time in a long while, I actually noticed how I felt at all. It was an exquisite, albeit fleeting, feeling.

All my body wanted to do was go home and get a good night's rest. But, as usual, I ignored the calling. I went to the bathroom to change my clothes and, just like Wonder Woman, zipped up my red, knee-high, Fluevog boots, practically flipped my cape over my shoulder, and strutted over to the fancy hotel. Despite not feeling very superhero-y that evening, I walked through the hotel lobby with a smile painted on my face—immigrit.

Nate's sister was waiting for me at a small table for two in the hotel lounge. We chatted for a while, ordered a drink, and caught up. Suddenly, out of nowhere, Nate popped out from behind her.

Shocked, I exclaimed, "What are you doing here?"

"I drove in to have dinner with you," he replied.

"Oh," I said without too much enthusiasm, a little bewildered.

His sister got up and said, "Okay, I have to go home. Have a great night."

What? I was confused. *We're staying here?* While having dinner in Edmonton wasn't uncommon for us, the fancy hotel seemed a bit much for our taste. And now we had two cars in the city? Bad planning, I thought, but went with it.

Dinner was a bit of a blur. I wasn't very hungry, considering I had been at an Ayurveda cooking class all day, eating and tasting food. So, when asked if I wanted dessert, I declined. To my dismay, they brought it out anyway. The server set down a beautifully plated dessert in front of me, with a giant, bright-red rose on top and, at the very center… a stunning platinum-band diamond ring.

My mouth dropped open. The sounds of the restaurant, the voices, the clinking of glasses—all began to blur together. Nate said something that didn't quite fully register then asked, "Will you marry me?"

I looked at him—this kind, lovable man with whom I'd spent my entire adult life and who I'd found *comfort* in like no other. I furrowed my brow, crinkled my nose, and, after a pause, blurted, "Are you sure?"

Yep.

Are. You. Sure.

Those were the three words that came out of my mouth after this man had just driven three hours on Death Road to surprise me, created a decoy plan with his family, booked an expensive suite and dinner at the fanciest hotel in the city, and proposed marriage.

He smiled, chuckled lightly, and responded, "Yes, I'm sure."

I nodded slowly and said, "Okay, yes."

The servers burst into applause. The rest of the night was a big, messy blur. And I mean messy. After tasting food all day, drinks, a four-course meal, and now a marriage proposal, my stomach was in turmoil. When we got up to our suite, I rushed past the rose petals, the hearts, and the champagne, straight into the ensuite bathroom, where I promptly stuck my head in the porcelain bowl and vomited the very expensive meal I had just eaten.

It's safe to say the typical reaction to a marriage proposal is joy—uncontainable excitement even. But not for me. Nope. This girl found it difficult to contain her meal.

Reluctantly, I slipped into one of the many dresses Nate had thoughtfully chosen for me and forced myself to go back downstairs to the lobby for a celebratory drink—immigrit.

The furthest thing from comfortable, that night felt like an out-of-body experience, and one I chalked up to "eating too much." However, in hindsight, it was far more than that. I was literally saying "yes" to things that didn't feel right for me at the time. My body was saying "no," but, as usual, I ignored it. I had literally asked, "Are you sure?" out loud, and maybe, just maybe, I was asking myself to pause and reflect.

But I didn't pause. Nor reflect. I just kept going. Full speed ahead. What followed was a whirlwind of epic wedding planning. Since I was waiting for my new yoga studio to be built, wedding planning conveniently became my new full-time job—immigrit.

Honestly, I'm not big on marriage. Commitment? Sure. Marriage? Meh. I hadn't dreamt about my wedding day or the man of my dreams since I was a little girl. Nate and I hadn't seriously discussed marriage, and I wasn't sure I even believed in the institution of it. I wasn't religious, I wasn't lonely, and at thirty-four, my uterus still wasn't interested in renting its space out to another human. So, marriage wasn't a very high priority on my bucket list.

But weddings? That's another story. When I plan an event, I *PLAN. AN. EVENT.* It was also no mistake that it took nine months, from marriage proposal to wedding day, for me to plan the wedding. It was a gestation period that birthed an elaborate three-day, indoor-outdoor, multicultural, multi-event "wedding of the century" (as one friend called it) in none other than my natural backyard oasis on the lake.

While the wedding itself was a fantastical flurry of color, sound, ceremony, family, and friends, being married was almost the opposite. Being married felt, well, comfortable. Something within me settled (including my stomach), and while I can't deny I still had doubts leading up to the wedding, something also felt safe about marrying my friend, Nate. And, as friends do, they grow. It seems friends either grow together or grow apart, and in our case, Nate and I had done both during the three and a half years after our wedding.

Nate loved being social and I loved sharing meals with people, so our home naturally became a central social hub, a.k.a. Party Central. Our peaceful place quickly filled with vibrant meals, conversations, drinks, and people. Lots and lots of people. In fact, all three of our wedding anniversaries were celebrated with at least one other person in tow, which neither of us seemed to mind. In fact, I think we both preferred it that way.

On our third wedding anniversary, in 2011, we sat down for a romantic dinner for two, only to realize the conversation wasn't flowing nearly as well as the wine was. Without saying too much, we just looked at each other, both thinking the same thing. We ended up inviting a few of our friends to join us for our "romantic" anniversary meal.

Yes, it was rare for Nate and me to be home alone. Our house was full of people almost all of the time. Whether people came to our place to be in nature, do yoga, eat, drink, stay, or party, our home ended up being a retreat for many different people in many different ways. And I trust it served each person exactly as they needed it to. When I saw that house on the lake for the first time, I knew it was the "retreat" I had asked for years before, back when my colleague had asked me what I wanted to do outside of teaching. Serendipitously, that same colleague ended up visiting our home on the lake. After exploring the home and the property, she cupped my face and whispered, "Your wellness retreat... You found it."

For me, it was a healing haven, a sanctuary, a creative outlet, and, yes, an abundant space for my craft, my ideas, and of course lots and lots of parties. With so many social gatherings, alcohol was also a constant presence. And not just at our house. Throughout the town, alcohol was available at every gathering, sporting event, and outdoor activity. It was part of the unwritten rule for knitting together the social fabric of the community. For me, the wine culture soon became my drug of choice, too.

I spent years numbing out with alcohol. It was the perfect distraction, a way to avoid tough conversations and heavy feelings. The more I drank, the less I cared, and the more careless I became, the further I distanced myself from those who truly cared about me.

Carelessness became my defense mechanism, my way of avoiding vulnerability and intimacy. Growing up, I was often called "careless" by my mom, a label that only reinforced my sense of emotional detachment. By nature, I cared deeply, but when that care wasn't reciprocated or appreciated, I swung to the opposite side, shutting myself off. This pendulum swing between caring and careless was my way of protecting myself from feeling hurt, rejected, or wrong. Carelessness was the armor I slapped on to protect myself from another Buster Brown betrayal at all costs. "I don't care" became part of my vernacular and being called "careless" actually started to feel like a compliment to me.

At first, being careless felt freeing—especially when I was around people like Nate, whose carefree attitude was so different from what I had known. It felt like a breath of fresh air. But over time, I realized that my carelessness—fueled by alcohol—was just another way I was abandoning myself. I was ignoring my own boundaries, numbing out, and distancing myself from my emotions, all while convincing myself it was "freedom." It took a toll on my relationships, my health, and my sense of self. I was a walking juxtaposition. A living breathing incongruence.

I was teaching wellness. My body was strong, fit, and flexible. I had cared for my body excessively for most of my life, but after saying goodbye to the vibrant, healthy, caring Serena in the mirror that day six years ago, I stopped caring what I put in it or on it or what it needed. I dimmed myself down as best I could—hiding behind baggy clothes, red wine, and a smile.

Inside, though, I was miserable. My inner smallness was a direct result of my outer a lot-ness. I drank a lot, skipped meals a lot, exercised a lot, worked a lot, and stayed up late a lot. I treated my body like a machine without ever taking it in for repair. And even though I felt tired, overwhelmed, and resentful, I kept going—immigrit.

Until I couldn't anymore.

Even though I felt indestructible, alcohol proved to be one of the most destructive forces in my life. Noticing more and more how alcohol influenced my deep unproductivity, I started to curtail my habits. I chose to be the designated driver, so I could leave and come home early. I went to bed before everyone left my house. I even stopped going out altogether.

As I began to cut back on alcohol and shift my focus to other areas of my life, I started to notice the growing distance between Nate and me. He started coming home later and later and, sometimes, not at all. Partly because we were interested in different things, and partly because I had been avoiding true connection—not just with him, but with myself.

One afternoon, Nate and I were sitting together on our back deck. I was lost in my own lonely thoughts, my gaze fixed on the shimmering lake, but I wasn't really seeing it. My mind was elsewhere, trapped in memories of a different time. It reminded me of when I would stare out the window of my classroom, lost in daydreams about something more, something beyond the confines of my life. It was happening again. But this time, it wasn't four classroom walls in which I felt restricted, it was the smallness of the town where I lived that had limited my big dreams for something more—something I couldn't quite imagine just yet.

At that time, I had just finished teaching my thirty-eighth class of the week, and Nate had just won his second term as town councilor. It was a win for him, but I felt a deep personal loss. Everyone around us was celebrating his victory, while I was alone at home, silently weeping.

He had added another community service responsibility to his already full plate at the group home, and I knew what lay ahead for me, for us. Another four years of the same thing. Even the prospect of it left me feeling burned out.

I had said "Yes" to too many things I didn't really want to commit to, and in doing so, I had created a life that once brought me satisfaction but now left me empty and exhausted. It was no longer sustainable. I couldn't keep living this way, trapped in a small town on the edge of the lake, stuck on an endless cycle of burnout and numbness. It wasn't the life I wanted anymore.

From the first day we met, Nate had clearly sensed my exotic birdness. He would always say, "I never want to stand in your way." And he never did.

In truth, *I* was the one who always managed to stand in my own way. Winona, along with my immigrit, kept me incongruent and tangled in the struggle for way too long. Nate and I had pushed and pulled the fabric of our relationship together and apart so much, it could no longer hold us together, and we eventually fell apart. I had walled up my heart, left my body, puked up my gut feelings, and ignored the red flags (and direct messages) I had gotten from people, animals, my body, and bumper stickers.

But now, it was time to listen. Time to trust the persistent tug in my heart that had been pulling me away from this life, from this town. There was more out there for me, far beyond the confines of that lake.

And just like that, we began the difficult conversation of going our separate ways. Nate set this exotic bird free.

***

Six months later, in 2012, I found myself sitting on my favorite olive-green leather chaise, facing the large picture window. The separation was now real—Nate was staying in the downstairs bedroom for convenience, while I lived upstairs. I had promised my students I'd give them six months to complete their class passes before closing my yoga studio and leaving Deer Lake for good. There were only a couple of days left before the transition was final.

I had spent weeks sorting through boxes, unsure of what to pack, torn between keeping some things or leaving them behind. As I gazed out across the calm, glassy lake one last time, the message from my squirrel spirit guide swept through my mind: *Change is coming. Store the necessary provisions for the long journey ahead.*

In the stillness of my home, the finality of the separation settled in—an ending to a chapter of my life that had spanned sixteen years, my entire adult life at that point. As I sat with the enormity of it all, I was struck by the uncertainty of my future. There was a certain gravity in that uncertainty, a heaviness in knowing I was not only leaving a marriage, I was stepping into a vast unknown. I had no clear path ahead, only the instinct to move forward, and I didn't know where I was going or what I would do when I got there. It was the hardest kind of freedom—one that required me to let go of the comfort I had once valued so deeply.

I got up from the chaise to make myself a cup of tea. As I passed the kitchen island, my fingers brushed along the handcrafted stained-concrete countertop. I filled my bright-red Le Creuset kettle with water and grabbed my favorite handcrafted pottery mug. With both hands, I hugged it close to my chest and paused to take in the inspirational creative space that held so many beautiful memories.

After word spread that Nate and I were splitting up, our once-bustling home was radio silenced. A house that had once been full of human voices and screams of laughter was now... crickets. People I had once considered friends vanished into thin air overnight. At a time when I needed a friend the most, I found myself all alone. Except for Nate himself.

In the end, Nate and I were friends who still wanted the best for each other. But after sixteen years together, we were no longer at our best. We consciously uncoupled—making a promise not to speak poorly of one another—and accepted our karma together was complete. (Or at least that's how I explained my imminent divorce to my disenchanted immigrant parents, who, as expected, saw it as a shameful failure.)

When a bird and a fish fall in love, it's beautiful, but where do they live, indeed? The rope that had tethered this exotic bird to the lake for so long was frayed and weathered. It was time for me to spread my wings, expand my horizons, and liberate myself from the nest I had created on the edge of a lake in a little northern town. It was time for this bird to fly, leave the nest for good, and let the fish frolic freely in the lake without her.

"EEEEEEEEEE..."

My thoughts were interrupted by the comforting whistle of the kettle on the stove. I poured the boiling water into my mug, swirled in some tulsi chai, held the steaming cup up to my face, closed my eyes, and inhaled deeply. And suddenly, it hit me. As if the hot steam had melted away the armor of carelessness I had wrapped around myself. I realized I had invested everything I had into something I was about to walk away from—with nothing more than a few boxes of clothes, a blender, and a heart full of memories. I was leaving a sixteen-year relationship, a thriving business, and a home I loved. This would be the last time I'd enjoy a cup of tea in my sanctuary on the lake, the last time I'd sleep in my comfy king-size bed, and the last time I'd teach class to a community that had come to mean so much to me. The reality sank in: my life as I knew it was crumbling, slipping away into insignificance. And so was I.

I hadn't cried much, but just then, the dam broke. I thumped the mug down, sloshing tea on the counter, and burst into tears. Crumpling to the ground, I crawled over to the rug in the living room, curled into a ball, hugged myself tightly, and bawled.

My inconsolable cries were so loud, Nate rushed upstairs to see what was happening. When he saw me lying in a fetal position on the floor, sobbing uncontrollably, he did the only thing a good friend would do. He lay down beside me, held me close, and cried with me.

Chapter 13
LAND OF ENTRAPMENT

DIVORCE IS LIKE STANDING at the threshold of the dream home you built from the ground up and watching the door slam shut in your face. Directionless and disoriented, starting again seems daunting.

What we don't realize in that moment, however, is that when a door closes, a window opens somewhere. And after a disillusioned ending, it's a matter of finding the window with a more aligned view to your new beginning.

My more aligned new beginning began when I decided to fully embrace my yogi uncle's advice—to *be* yoga. And since Ayurveda was the closest thing to making me feel like I was actually living yoga, I knew it was time for the deep dive. So, at the end of 2012, I closed the door to my life in Deer Lake, and this free bird spread her wings and flew out the open window and across the border to California to study, practice, and live Ayurveda. Thus began the inward journey to myself.

Studying Ayurveda full time wasn't just about deepening my understanding of this ancient science in order to expand my professional skill set and hone my craft. On a subconscious level, it was my way to recover from burnout, process ending my marriage, and set things in motion for the next chapter of my life.

After exhausting all my resources, it was my turn to be held, nurtured, and cared for. Over the next four years, I outsourced healers, visionaries, luminaries, therapists, teachers, Vedic astrologers, naturopaths, Chinese and Ayurvedic medicine doctors—basically, anyone and everyone who could help me heal and grow. I found solace, self-care, and growth in yoga studios in California, retreat centers in Massachusetts, meditation ashrams in Quebec, research centers in India, Vedic astrologers in Switzerland, and hidden gems in the mountain ranges of New Mexico.

Ayurveda teaches that we are a mirror reflection of our environment, and I can honestly say I never felt healthier or more in tune with myself than during those four years. I went to bed and woke up early, shopped at local food co-ops and farmer's markets, quit drinking alcohol, and studied yoga and Ayurveda with some of the top leaders in the industry. I had found *my people* and resourced myself happily. While I felt replenished and often wore a permagrin that wouldn't wipe off, I also embarked on an enormous, sometimes painful undertaking of transformation—one that often brought sudden waves of grief and countless tears.

I cried on the yoga mat, in meditation, in ceremony, in class, on hikes, at festivals, on planes, and even on the subway. For four years, I traveled, grieved, and healed—and I did it alone. Immigrit. On a ten-day silent retreat based on the meditative practice of the late guru or teacher, Swamiji Goenka, which involved no talking, no eye contact, no reading, and no writing, all I had left to do was cry.

SERENA ARORA

Most people who knew me back then might not have believed I could handle ten days of silence. But the truth was, my body craved it. It soaked up the stillness, savored the peace, and thrived as a result. I was asleep by 9:00 p.m., woke at 4:00 a.m. without an alarm, ate two meals a day, and had fruit and herbal tea for dinner. My digestion and elimination were strong, my mood steady and calm, and I was deeply content. During breaks from meditation, I'd walk outside and have full conversations in my head—with trees, toads, and birds. It reminded me of similar chats I had with myself during those long bike rides as a kid.

Halfway through the retreat, we had the option to meditate in our rooms rather than in the large meditation hall. I was staying in a dorm with five other women, each bed separated by free-standing dividers. Just before the 4:30 morning gong signaled meditation time, I poked my head under the dividers to find the room empty—no feet or legs. Everyone had gone to the hall (or so I thought), so I decided to stay back.

As soon as I closed my eyes, the tears came. My normally statuesque meditative posture softened, and I gave myself permission to release what I'd been holding in for too long.

In the midst of my sniffling, I heard a voice. I hadn't heard a human voice in five days, so it seemed extra loud, reverberating through the dorm room.

"Don't keep it in. It's good to let it go."

I opened my eyes and quickly looked under the room dividers once more. There was still no sign of any other human. Was this someone in spirit form, then?

"Swamiji?" I said out loud, confused but wondering if this was my late guru's voice.

UNBOUND

I waited. No response. After a moment of silence, and in true meditative form, I let go of analyzing from where the sound came. Perhaps it was a roommate who had stayed back that day; perhaps it was the late guru's spirit. In any case, I did let go, silently thanked them, closed my eyes, and cried some more.

By Day Ten, I felt free.

Next, I dove into Ayurveda through both traditional gurukulam-style (a residential school under the guidance of a guru or teacher) study and formal college program of study in Northern California. Fortuitously, I stayed with my cousin, the son of my yogi uncle, and his lovely wife—who just happened to cook the most delicious Indian food. It couldn't be more fitting that it was my yogi uncle's son who generously opened his home to me for four months, providing a place where I could truly *be* yoga. Grateful, I could hear my yogi uncle's voice from across the world, "Okay, good, beta. Good. Finally. Now *be* yoga."

Sitting on the floor among my Ayurvedic peers, we crowded around the renowned Ayurvedic doctor and teacher, Dr. Vasant Lad, who had flown in from New Mexico to teach us that weekend. While most of the students were starstruck, I had no idea who he was or what he had accomplished, which made for some interesting interactions between us.

Like the time when he drew intricate diagrams on the whiteboard. After he erased them, I blurted out, "Dr. Lad, your drawings are incredible. You should really put them in a book."

The class fell silent. One student nudged me strongly, leaned over, and whispered in my ear, "He's written a ton of books, and all his drawings are in there. He's famous!"

My heart sank with embarrassment, but Dr. Lad seemed genuinely amused by my innocent suggestion.

Or when he offered tongue readings to our class, a diagnostic tool in Ayurveda. When it was my turn, he stared at my tongue for what felt like hours (though it was only seconds). Peering at my gaping mouth through the bottom of his bifocals, he jutted his chin out and stared silently at my outstretched tongue.

Then, he finally announced in front of the entire class, "This is the best tongue I've seen." Thirty-five heads leaned in for a closer look.

Or when I asked if he would read my palm during a break, and he obliged. After holding my hand up to the light while sighing and bobbling his head side to side in typical yes-no Indian style for some time, he asked in his sweet Indian accent, "Do you *really* want to know the truth?"

"Um... Uh... Yes?" I stammered.

He nodded gravely, bobbled his head again, and said, "Okay. Just come to Albuquerque. Everything will be okay," and he wrote down a number on a slip of paper. "Call this number. They'll take care of it."

After thanking him, I walked back to my desk. I stared at the piece of paper, thinking, *Take care of what? And where the heck is Albuquerque?*

When I called the number and spoke with the Dean of Education, due to my previous formal training and experience in Ayurvedic health treatments, therapies, and philosophy, I was accepted into the final year of the Ayurvedic Institute's program before I even applied. Maybe Dr. Lad told the Dean about my palm reading. Or maybe the Universe just knew this was what I needed. Either way, I bought Dr. Lad's "famous books," and packed them in my car, and drove a thousand miles east, to Albuquerque, New Mexico.

Ah, New Mexico. The Land of Enchantment. Also known to some as the land of "entrapment." It's quickly understood that New Mexico will teach you something about yourself, if you're willing to listen and learn, and you'll never leave the same.

I had much to learn, though more about myself than Ayurveda. And Dr. Lad, of course, knew this. My first lesson came during our initial clinical class, when Dr. Lad brought me up to the front of the room to demonstrate medical palpation and pulse.

He turned to me and said to the class, "I met you in California, isn't it?"

"Yes, Dr. Lad, you did," I replied with a smile.

He turned to the rest of the students and said, "She is a very bright, brilliant student." Then, he carried on with the demonstration. I remember very distinctly not being able to receive his compliment, that something inside me didn't believe him. And Dr. Lad knew I hadn't.

If you know anything about Dr. Lad, you understand he brought me up to the front of the class and carefully curated his comment with the intention of teaching me something about myself, not medical palpation. It worked. I don't remember much about palpation, but I certainly remember how I felt in that moment. Thank you, Dr. Lad.

While I loved being a student again, and Ayurveda felt second nature to me, at age forty, I was one of the oldest students in my class. So, when the young twenty-something millennials in my class invited me to a full-moon ceremony one Friday evening, I was delighted. I had no idea what to expect and had absolutely no clue what a full-moon ceremony entailed, but I was willing to find out. That Friday evening, I was about to enter a whole new realm.

When I walked into the house, nine girls were sitting in a circle on the living room floor with candles, flowers, crystals, journals, statues, and deities all strategically placed in the middle of the circle. I couldn't help but think, *Aw, they're so cute.* While I studied textbooks and memorized facts, these girls held hands and burned sage. They believed the Universe would guide their spiritual journey and made decisions according to the alignment of the planets. I couldn't even name all the planets, let alone let them plan my week and my wardrobe.

As I moved through the room, I felt like I was in a foreign language class. Conversations revolved around the Universe, feminine energy, the moon, its cycle, and their own moon cycles. I had no language for any of this. It took me a while to even realize that they were talking about their periods; I was even more surprised to learn how much reverence and power it held.

I hadn't spoken about my period or really even thought about it since I was fourteen years old, let alone contemplate it in relation to the moon. I was the daughter of Asian immigrants whose parents came from a region of the world where taboos surrounding menstruation was common. I had lived in my head, doubted and repressed my feelings, and separated my body from my emotions my entire life. Whereas these girls lived and acted from their hearts, their guts, and their wombs.

As I awkwardly navigated my way through the room, I couldn't help but feel out of place. But despite being out of my element, I stayed open. It was Friday night, I had just moved to a new state, I lived alone, and these young ladies seemed sweet. Not only were these girls serious about ethereal matters, they were seriously passionate about them, and after a while, I found it enlightening.

Then, one of the girls pulled out a shiny silver machete. *Okay, maybe they aren't as sweet as I thought.*

Another girl called the room to attention. As the girl held the machete lovingly in her hands, she explained how it was a gift from an old curandera, a medicine woman. She invited us to use it in the ceremony as a physical symbol to help release energetic cords that kept us tied to the past. We'd cut those cords with the machete to make space for new growth. These girls had been around the block, or rather the moon, and weren't messing around: they clearly knew something I didn't.

Each girl said a few words, reflecting on what she was letting go of. Then, she took the machete and, in one fell swoop, cut her invisible energetic cord, which she felt held her back from moving forward in her life, while the others witnessed and held space for her. I was fascinated by what I was seeing and hearing. Just like that, these sweet young girls transformed into some of the most powerful women I had ever been in the presence of.

It was my turn. One of the girls handed me the machete, and all eyes turned toward me.

I knew what I had to release. I had known for a while now. It was the one thing I knew deep down but was too afraid to admit. Even though Nate and I had been separated for over two years, something still felt like it was hanging on. With one last remaining frayed thread between us, I realized it was time. It was time to cut the line, remove the hook, and release the fish back into the lake for good. It was time to cut the tie to my past, to the safety of comfort, to what felt familiar, and to the aching guilt that it could have been different.

I slowly slid one hand at a time down the long silver shaft of the machete, gripped the handle carefully with both hands, and raised it up over my head. I breathed deeply, closed my eyes, and released the grip of the past. I said the words that had been sitting heavily on my heart for too long, opened my eyes, and with an instinctive primal exhale, swung it with a fierceness that I had never felt before.

It felt like I was finally setting myself free. And then, something from the very darkest corner of my energetic heart space broke open. A wave of emotion swept over me, and I surrendered to the most raw emotional state I had felt since lying on the floor in a fetal position two years prior.

I dropped to the floor and wept while these young women witnessed my vulnerable unraveling. Eyes closed, I felt something strangely pointy pressing down on my thigh.

I opened my tear-filled eyes to see a cat standing in my lap. A *cat*? I hadn't seen a cat in the house earlier. I was allergic to cats and not a fan of felines, so my first instinct was to push it off of me. But, for whatever reason, that's not what I did.

Instead, I did the exact opposite. I placed my hand on the cat's head and, very uncharacteristically of me, started to stroke its gray fur. For several minutes, I just sat there, crying and petting the cat, who was now curled up in my lap. I instantly felt settled, and the next time I opened my eyes, the cat was nowhere to be found.

When the ceremony was over, one of the young girls came up to me and, in a quiet voice, said as a matter-of-factly, "It was so powerful, Serena. I saw it all happen. After you sliced the cord, you healed right up immediately." She circled her hand in the air in front of my abdomen. "And then," she continued, "the cord snapped away from you and coiled up at his feet." She pointed somewhere far off, away from me.

I'd hardly shared a word about my marriage with any of them. In fact, I hadn't shared much about myself at all. However, not only did she seem to know, she said it with utter certainty. And even though Nate was far away, he'd still apparently received the message loud and clear.

She was right.

The very next day, straight out of a tragic romcom, Nate called me out of the blue. We hadn't been talking very often lately, so the greeting was a little clunky at first. After a few pleasantries, he finally said the thing we had both been actively avoiding. "It came in the mail. The divorce is final."

That call was powerful proof that there's a higher force at play—the Universe. The ceremony woke me up to the fact that I still have so much to learn. I also found out the cat didn't belong to anybody in the house and that nobody had a clue where it came from or how it even got into the house. And if that weren't strange enough, I didn't get even a hint of an allergic reaction that night. Yep, this machete-cutting, spirit-animal, full-moon-ceremony stuff is really... out of this world!

That night, my heart had cracked open, and I was finally ready to hear what it had to say. I had been bound to the comfort of Nate, the ideal of a lasting marriage, and the cultural stigma to divorce. This single traditional strand of guilt kept me from moving forward and making room for something (and someone) new in my more aligned life.

And so, my heart was urging me to write a letter. A letter to the Universe. A letter to my future beloved. I hadn't written a letter to anybody asking for anything in my life, let alone to the Universe. But with my newfound trust in the moon and such, what did I have to lose?

I knew what I didn't want, but did I know what I wanted? *Be yoga, Serena. Be yoga*, I repeated to myself on behalf of my yogi uncle, as I twirled the pen around in my hand. I slowed down, stopped thinking, and let my pen do the talking.

"Dear beloved," it started writing, "I know that you have been waiting patiently for me to cut the cord from my past. To heal and move forward. Thanks for your patience. I'm ready now..."

In the letter, I asked my beloved to come find me when we were both ready. The partner who is a match for me, who knows who he is and owns his place in this world. Who has lived a similar path as I have and who is self-assured yet humble, successful yet generous, strong yet sensitive, secure, sexy and... not gassy. Oh, and I want to be *ravished*."

After that first full-moon ceremony weekend in New Mexico in 2012, I became a believer in something higher. Something much more powerful and intuitive than my own tiny human head could ever conjure up. And, unbeknownst to me at the time, this was the beginning of a long, challenging spiritual journey back to my heart. A painful journey of self-discovery and transformation that would include many more ceremonies, letter-writing, spirit animals, full moons, and full-circle moments. And like so many others, I had entered the Land of Entrapment as a young girl, and now I'd emerged as a woman who would never be the same again.

Chapter 14
OUT OF GAS

TWO YEARS AFTER THAT fateful full-moon ceremony, I was still living and teaching in New Mexico. I slowly inched my black Acura, Babs, into the middle of a busy Albuquerque intersection, waiting to turn left. My eyes were fixed on the gas gauge that had been teetering on dangerously low for days. My heart was racing, and the click of the turn signal hammered in my head like a ticking time bomb.

Praying my car wouldn't stall in the middle of traffic, I slapped the dashboard and yelled out loud, *"C'mon, Babs! You can do it, girl! Just get to the other side!"*

Searching desperately for an opening in traffic, I slammed my foot down on the gas pedal. It clicked.

I was completely out of gas.

Panic surged as I jammed my foot repeatedly into the unresponsive gas pedal.

"C'mon, Babs, *c'mon!*" I shouted.

Riding on only fumes, Babs crawled painfully across two lanes of oncoming traffic, barely slipping past the next wave of honking vehicles. Then, she drifted toward the curb and slid across two empty parking spots in the corner CVS parking lot before completely conking out.

SERENA ARORA

Wide-eyed and white-knuckled (which isn't easy for this brown girl with Asian eyes to be), I dropped my forehead onto the steering wheel with a dull thud. Adrenaline surged through me as my heart pounded furiously in my stomach. But I was relieved Babs and I had made it out unscathed, so I shook my head in disbelief. And then, immigrit ensued as I proceeded to scold myself unrelentingly.

"*Goddammit*, girl! You could've been seriously hurt. What the hell were you thinking, waiting for days to get gas? *What*? You really thought you'd make it? You've been running on empty for so long! Too long. Too fucking long. So, wake up, because time's up! It was up a long time ago, and if you don't do something about it soon, you won't be so lucky next time."

I wasn't just talking about the near accident I had just experienced or even about Babs. I was referring to my own metaphorical gas tank, which had been running on empty for the last year. Although I was in a new place, my pattern of doubt, over-giving, resentment, and burnout had come along for the ride.

After graduating as an Ayurvedic Health Practitioner from the Institute, I was asked to return the following year to teach Ayuryoga to first- and second-year Ayurveda students. It felt like everything I had worked so hard for and a culmination of decades of study, combining my two passions, Ayurveda and yoga, while working alongside brilliant minds like Dr. Lad. I had spent a lifetime building up to this opportunity, my ultimate dream job.

Unfortunately for me, behind every dream was Winona, waiting in the wings, ready to sabotage that dream and turn it into a nightmare. Thus, while Albuquerque brought many wishes of mine to life, it also brought experiences that, while powerful in their own way, felt more like a bad dream I couldn't escape. Harsh, relentless, uncomfortable experiences, just like the dry, unyielding land of New Mexico itself.

That year, I had started out as a vibrant, juicy, freshly-divorced forty-year-old woman, eager to learn and ready to take on the world. I was also ripe for the picking—especially for those who desired my juiciness for themselves, like thirsty hyenas drawn to a desert oasis.

One particularly parched hyena cub was lured to my watery boundaries in the Albuquerque high desert that year—Yogi Boy. And Winona, along with my needy relationship pattern, allowed my juicy self to be sucked completely dry and me to become a shriveled husk of the vibrant woman I once was.

After the dissolution of my marriage and life as I knew it, Winona came back. And this time with a vengeance. She wanted to prove to me and others that I was still lovable, still desirable, and still worthy of being chosen. So, her go-to strategy of pursuing and "winning" something or someone made Yogi Boy the perfect target. He needed fuel (mine), and I needed validation.

Yogi Boy was the complete opposite of Nate. He was into yoga, Ayurveda, and spiritual pursuits. He was also young, lost, and craved to be mothered. And while I had proclaimed at a young age I would never be anybody's maid, mistress, or mother, Yogi Boy came to test that last proclamation. Hard. And he won.

Mothering Yogi Boy came painfully easily to me, at forty. My watery boundaries, combined with my culturally honed skills for appeasing, pleasing, and sacrificing my needs in exchange for love, made me easy prey. Yogi Boy brought out the sixteen-year-old wounded teenager in me who was used to over-giving, tolerating disrespect, and being blind to red flags.

I gave generously, doting on Yogi Boy unconditionally, and abandoned myself in the process, robbing me of my integrity, dignity, and power. I mothered the hell out of Yogi Boy. And I expected appreciation in return, which of course I didn't get, leaving me to feel resentful and ashamed. I considered myself a smart, savvy woman, and yet I found myself stripped bare at forty years old, exposing my teenage wounds of self-doubt, self-abandonment, and devalued self-worth to the world. I was the ideal candidate to cater to wounded hyenas and their unmet childhood needs.

While this high-desert hyena's thirst was quenched by my tending, I spiraled into a dark, depressed, codependent hole.

With Yogi Boy, I relived my high-school-boy experience, twenty-five years later, and I later learned this experience was a karmic debt I had to repay. So, while the Yogi Boy relationship proved draining, I also knew, if I didn't face the lesson this time, it would surely revisit me again, and maybe even louder next time. And so, vulnerable and trusting in fate, I faced my karmic debt head-on... and let it kick my ass.

I shed layer upon layer until my four-year-old girl was left with nothing but an opportunity to heal her deepest Buster-Brown wound. A once-ripe and juicy fruit had turned into a hardened, crispy tumbleweed, drifting aimlessly across the vast New Mexican desert, until, one day, I ran out of gas in the middle of a busy intersection. My debt finally repaid, I woke up from my nightmare in that CVS parking lot.

And so, I swung to the opposite end of the pleasing pendulum. Instead of saying "yes" without discernment, I entered a phase of saying No. To everything and anything that left me feeling empty, depleted, and drained. (Yogi Boy was the first to go.)

And then there was immigrit.

Immigrit's only goal is to get to the other side, void of feelings, empathy, and patience, while leaving wounds in its wake. I was so steeped in immigrit, I didn't realize that I had subconsciously used it to stay with Yogi Boy in order to get to the other side of my karmic debt. And, because I was so infused with immigrit, I ignored and buried the emotions that came along with doing that.

Immigrit and Winona are a lethal combination that left my head and my heart in a veritable tug-of-war. And since my cultural upbringing prioritizes brain intellect over emotional intelligence, my heart had been on mute for decades. It took a CVS parking lot wakeup call loud enough to silence Winona in order to reawaken my heart.

And then, I started doing something unheard of to a daughter of immigrants. I asked my heart what it felt and then actually listened for an answer. Not only was listening to my heart unfamiliar and uncomfortable for me, my heart had been quiet for so long, sometimes it took a long time for an answer to come. Sometimes, it never came at all. Instead of spontaneously saying "yes" to something or someone, I waited to make a decision until I was certain that my best interests were at heart. (Thanks, but no thanks, Winona.)

I started saying *yes* to my own needs with discernment. "Yes" to certain people, projects, and places that felt fulfilling, nourishing, and aligned. I would start sentences with "I feel," instead of "I think" and built boundaries from the ground up. And, although it took a lot of effort and time before I felt safe enough to listen to, empathize with, and trust what my heart had to say, my heart began to speak loudly.

I also started doing something else I had never done before. Instead of allowing immigrit to blindly bulldoze its way through my life, I *redirected* it. I relied on the *tenacity* of immigrit to rebuild my strength, stamina, and vitality. I used the *bravery* of immigrit to create firm, unwavering boundaries strong enough to protect my ever-growing reservoir of energy.

I even used someone else's immigrit to refuel my empty tank. A generous friend in Albuquerque, imbued with her own South Asian immigrit, used hers to chisel away at the scar tissue of my old wounds. She used the *persistence* of her immigrit to get me through this pivotal intersection, like I did for Babs: "C'mon, love, you can do it! Just get to the other side!" she'd say to me—immigrit squared.

My work has been to practice staying in the middle of the pendulum swing, making empowered decisions that are in my best interest. Decisions with discernment that come from my heart, not my head—where Winona still lives, by the way, but she's just quieter these days.

To be honest, this process of being patient with my heart, feeling my emotions, and articulating them in a way that lands has been challenging and messy. I still struggle to keep Winona from showing up from time to time, because she's a feisty one. Keeping her in the backseat or sending her to the back of the bus, to sit with all the other know-it-all sixth graders with senioritis, hasn't been easy. It also took me a long time to forgive myself—the girl, the teenager, and the woman who allowed (even caused) Winona to take the wheel for all those years.

I finally understood that, in order to liberate myself from Winona, I had to actually *thank* her for showing up. She showed up for me when I didn't. So, I had to give *her* the "win" for attempting to keep me safe in her own way. I had to thank her for protecting me, jumping to my rescue, and not wanting me to get hurt again.

And while it didn't always end well, like all the other scared women in my life I had to acknowledge her for doing the best she could with what she knew. I know better now and had to remind her I was now fully capable of driving my own life bus, that I was safe and she wasn't needed anymore. Learning to parent Winona first, and then myself, was essential for growing up and maturing into the embodied woman I knew myself to be.

I believe the Universe sent me to New Mexico to intensely play out my core pattern in a condensed period of time. Albuquerque is a powerful place, where harsh environments reveal hard lessons. It's where I found myself both hurt and healed, exposed and embraced, tested and transformed. I was forever changed by the high desert, and New Mexico will always hold a special place in my heart.

After writing "not gassy" in my letter to the Universe and then running out of gas in the middle of a busy intersection, I've come to understand that the Universe often gives you what you ask for and almost always what you need. So, be careful what you ask for. Be specific, and be prepared for the Universe's sometimes twisted sense of humor.

SERENA ARORA

I'm quite certain that Dr. Lad knew New Mexico was exactly what I needed when he read my palm that day. And while he likely knew it would be gut-wrenching, he was right: "Everything will be okay."

Chapter 15
CAASAA SOMBRIIIA

I HAD BEEN LEADING YOGA teacher trainings and traveling internationally to support students in becoming yoga teachers for over thirteen years at this point in 2016. I was still based in New Mexico, and direct flights from Houston airport made it easy for me to travel all over the world.

And travel, I did. In fact, I was fortunate enough to travel so often, the airport customs agents in Houston recognized me. Whenever they saw me in line, one of them would shout out loud to the others, "Hey! It's Yoga Girl!"

This time, I was heading to Costa Rica.

The first time I visited Costa Rica was in 1989, when I was fourteen years old. The country had just opened its borders to Canada, and as an avid traveler, my mom booked us on one of the first chartered flights out.

I remember stepping off the plane directly onto the tarmac, as Costa Rica's tourism was still in its infancy. I was instantly drenched, as if I had taken a shower with my clothes on, but I stood there in awe of this tropical paradise. The trip was a humid, sticky adventure that was, without a doubt, the most magical experience I'd had in my fourteen years. I fell in love with the natural world—the butterflies as large as birds, the leaves bigger than my torso, the monkeys howling like zombies in an apocalypse, and the giant sea turtles laboriously digging holes to lay their eggs in the wee morning hours.

When we got back home after our trip, I informed my mom of my plan. "Hey, Mom, in case you were wondering, I'm moving to Costa Rica." The conversation ended almost as quickly as it started.

As she crossed the room, she shot me her familiar dismissive look. "I'm not wondering. And no, you're not," she said in true immigrit fashion. "You're finishing high school, then you're going to university, then you're getting a job..." Her voice trailed off as she walked away. And that was that.

I ended up visiting Costa Rica many times after that—at age sixteen, on another family trip; at twenty-one, for my cousin's wedding; in my thirties, leading yoga teacher trainings and retreats. And now, here I was again, at forty-one.

Waiting in the customs line, I ran a hand through my disheveled hair, took a sip of water to clear my throat, and looked for my phone. A customs officer looked up, nodded at me, and gestured for me to step forward. He silently sized me up, extended his hand, and, without a word, I placed my open passport into it.

He thumbed through my well-worn passport, tapped at his computer, and asked in broken English, "Where you stay?"

"Oh, uh..." I fumbled through my phone to find the details of the retreat center where I was staying at. I had been teaching in Albuquerque and traveling so much, another teacher trainer and friend of mine, Isabel, had arranged the trip this time, and I was just showing up to teach. I found the information on my phone and replied, "Um. It's called Caasaa Sombrriiia."

Other than one semester of Beginner Spanish in university, my knowledge of the Spanish language and Latin countries was limited to ordering beer from a waiter and asking directions to the library. He paused, trying to read my lips, and repeated it back quickly, "Casa Sombria. How long?" he asked.

"Three weeks," I replied.

I hoped that would suffice. I didn't know much about the place, where it was, or how to get there. I just knew I was getting picked up at the airport and trusted that I'd arrive in one piece.

After asking a few more standard questions, the officer stamped my passport, and I headed to baggage claim. Each bag had been pulled off the conveyor belt and neatly grouped together on the floor: suitcases with suitcases, duffle bags with duffle bags, backpacks with backpacks— as though the bags themselves had spotted their familiar others from across the crowded room, jumped off the belt, crossed the culture chasm, and grouped themselves together by type. Even bags have immigrit.

I quickly spotted my suitcase among the sea of bags that snaked around the corner like dominoes. As I rolled it toward the main lobby, the sliding glass doors parted to announce my arrival.

I made my way toward a cluster of loud men near the entrance, all shouting, "Taxi! Taxi! *Hello! Taxi!*" and waving at me to get my attention. Having traveled extensively, I was used to this kind of airport mayhem and calmly scanned the crowd, looking for someone who would be holding a "Casa Sombria" sign.

Suddenly, a lean, dark-skinned man lunged toward me. He didn't have a sign, but he shouted, "I'm Jorge! I'll be your driver. Casa Sombria, right?"

How he knew I was the person he was looking for in the chaos of the airport and how I trusted he was who he said he was reminds me this was indeed a more trusting time in people and travel.

I opened the van window and let the warm, tropical evening breeze wash over me. Taking a deep breath, I felt that same exhilarating sense I always get when traveling—the smell of freedom. Jorge and I chatted the entire drive to Casa Sombria. It was getting dark, and the travel fatigue began to set in, but Jorge's old Mitsubishi Jeep kept me wide awake, bumping along those signature Costa Rican pothole-ridden gravel roads.

"Who" *clunk* "owns" *clank* "this place?" I asked between bumps. "An American?" *Slam!*

"No, he's Canadian," Jorge replied smoothly, clearly used to the bumpy roads.

My curiosity was piqued. I had lived in America for several years at that point, so Canada seemed a distant memory to me. Still, I asked, "Yeah? Who is he?"

"Callum," Jorge answered. "Good guy. Been living here for a while now. Yoga teacher. Divorced," he added casually, as if reading Callum's dating profile aloud.

It was dark when the Jeep finally stopped bouncing and pulled up to Casa Sombria. Jorge jumped out, grabbed my suitcase, and led me to my room. I thanked him, and he said he'd probably see me around, since he lived nearby and the town was small. I walked into my room and started to unpack and settle into what would be my home for the next twenty-one days.

The next morning, I woke up to the familiar sound of howler monkeys, as I had come to expect during my prior trips to Costa Rica. However, it was unseasonably warm—108°F—so I lay in bed, already sweaty at 6:00 a.m., taking in my new surroundings.

The ceiling fan spun lazily beneath the high vaulted ceilings. Dark wood beams stretched across the room, and stained-glass windows prismed the morning light. At the highest point of the room, a small mezzanine towered over the space below, complete with a tiny door leading somewhere—like something straight out of a fairytale, as though one of Snow White's seven dwarfs might step through it at any moment. I later discovered that this door led to a rooftop crow's nest, where lush green treetops and crimson sunsets made for a spectacular view.

As I lay there, my conversation with Jorge from the night before played over in my mind. *So, I thought to myself, the owner of this place is Canadian... And he teaches yoga... Callum... That name sounds so famili—*(gasp!) *Wait!*

Like a Google Map search, my brain, which had been picturing the vastness of Canada, zoomed over to the west, in on Alberta, then... yes, Calgary. I shot straight up in bed. *Oh, my gosh! I think I know this guy!* Well, I knew of him.

Five years before that very moment, I had been living on Struggle Street with Nate in Deer Lake. Searching for something to ease my mind, I had turned to Google. I don't quite remember exactly what I typed into the search engine, but I stumbled upon a YouTube video.

For sale was a custom-built, geothermal-heated home with a yoga studio on five acres in Caelmont, a bedroom community just south of Calgary. There was a promo video online. As I watched it, I remember thinking how "sales-y" the tall, White, tattooed, bald guy seemed, as he gave us a virtual tour of the property. Still, something about it kept drawing me back, and I watched the video several times.

I decided to call the realtor and arrange a visit the next time I was in Calgary. I toured the property three times—once by myself, once with my parents, and once with Nate. I still remember standing on the well-landscaped lawn with Nate.

He turned to me and said, "Why would I trade twenty-five acres on the lake for five acres on a pond?" And that was that. A few months later, we separated, I moved to California, and, well, you know the rest.

Now, five years later, there I was, sitting in that light-filled room in Costa Rica, nodding slowly to myself. I was definitely onto something. In the video, I remembered the tall, White, sales-y guy saying something about opening a yoga retreat in… Costa Rica! Could it be that, of all the (many) yoga retreat centers in Costa Rica, I had ended up at *his*? The guy from my hometown halfway across the world, whose YouTube video I had stumbled upon five years ago?

I shook my head to clear those thoughts and got ready for my day. When I went downstairs for breakfast, I started chatting with a colleague. And then, I saw him. The tall, White, tattooed, bald guy from the video, walked through the door directly behind her. Yep, it was him. It was "sales-y" guy.

Visibly distracted, I excused myself from the conversation and watched as he walked swiftly past the pool and toward the driveway. There was an assuredness in his step, a quiet confidence I had seen and felt in very few people, and suddenly, I felt a wave of intimidation wash over me. For a split second, I hesitated, almost deciding to turn back. But then the Universe nudged me gently forward. A confident voice within yelled, "You're Serena fucking Arora! Go introduce yourself."

I quickened my pace, rushed past the pool, and slipped through the gate into the driveway, calling out, "Callum?"

He stopped, turned around, and our eyes met. It was definitely him. As he saw me walking toward him, that wide-eyed, sales-y grin spread across his face.

"Hi," I said, offering a firm handshake. "I'm Serena, the other training facilitator. I almost bought your house five years ago in Caelmont."

His eyes flashed with recognition and confusion at the same time. As his eyebrows raised, a look of genuine curiosity spread across his face. Still holding my hand, he gazed at me for a moment before responding, "Wow, I haven't heard the word *Caelmont* in a long time."

We talked about Calgary, yoga studios on specific streets, and local teachers whom we both knew. Time seemed to slow down as we stood in the driveway in the sweltering heat, connecting over our shared past. Despite this being our first meeting, I felt like I had known him my entire life.

As I turned to head back past the pool, the tropical heat already seeping into my bones, I wiped beads of sweat from my lip and brow. It was going to be one hot training—in more ways than one.

Chapter 16
RAVISHED

I AM COMPLETELY IN my element when I'm training new, eager students, especially aspiring yoga teachers. I was enjoying this particular Casa Sombria training in Costa Rica, getting to know thirty-eight women—and Callum. Due to the heat, we started our days at 5:00 a.m. and gave the students a long break in the early afternoon, the hottest part of the day.

One week into the training, during a break, I checked my phone and saw a message from Callum: *I know you're busy, but I'd like to get to know you some.*

Jorge had been right about Callum. Not only was he a good guy, he was an astute, emotionally intelligent, highly communicative man—a rare breed in my relationship experience. I didn't often struggle to connect with people on the surface, but on a deeper more intimate level? That wasn't common for me, especially with a man. And especially with a man who, for whatever reason, piqued my interest.

Callum and I had a lot in common and never seemed to run out of things to talk about. We were both seasoned yoga teacher trainers who had lived and worked in similar circles and had even attended some of the same events, crossing paths but never meeting, until now. But there was more than that. We seemed to connect on a level I didn't quite understand yet.

In true immiguilt self-doubt style, I decided to turn to Isabel for some honest advice, asking her what she thought about me spending some time with Callum. Her response was more enthusiastic than I'd expected.

"Yes, do it! I really like Callum. He's been great to work with and seems like a stellar guy. Plus, it's not like you have much waiting for you back home." She flashed a gentle grin.

My mind drifted back to my life in Albuquerque. Being forty-one and single, my days were filled with going to group fitness classes at the gym, leading yoga teacher trainings, and collaborating on various projects with the quirky creatives who flocked to New Mexico.

I loved the up-and-coming foodie scene, which had earned Albuquerque the nickname "Little Portland" for its organic food co-ops, diverse markets, farm-to-table restaurants, food trucks, and handcrafted micro-breweries and meaderies. While there, I soaked up live music in unconventional grassroots venues, went to freethinking art festivals, cultural fiestas, open-mic speakeasies, the symphony, and the opera. I skied in Taos, soaked in hot springs in Santa Fe, marveled at monuments like White Sands and Tent Rocks, and danced at Red Rocks in Colorado. I was loving my life, my community, and myself fully, for the first time in my adult life.

I was renting a spacious loft on the edge of the downtown core with large picture windows and a top-floor balcony. With panoramic views of downtown Albuquerque, my unit was perched directly above a bustling café. Once the Albuquerque High School, it was now refurbished into what felt like a vibrant, diverse, safe community. It had a variety of housing options, and I was centrally located to everything. It was just a five-minute walk from some of my favorite restaurants, ten minutes to the airport, and only a short drive to Santa Fe, where I would escape every few weeks for exceptional yoga classes at Prajna Yoga, soak in the thermal pools at Ten Thousand Waves, and get my fill of South Indian food at Paper Dosa.

My days came alive at 5:00 a.m., when the commercial exhaust fan from the café below transformed my loft into what felt like a trembling airplane hangar. I felt electrified with the sounds of traffic, the occasional car backfiring (or maybe a gunshot—I could never quite tell), and the way downtown lit up like a Christmas tree every evening. One particular streetlamp shone directly through the floor-to-ceiling windows of my loft into my bedroom, as bright as the helicopter spotlight at the police raids that sometimes happened around nearby apartments. If you're familiar with the TV series *Breaking Bad*, you might know it was filmed in Albuquerque. After living there for four years, this location "casting" seemed fitting. I came to love the city's wild reputation, but also its unassuming and unfettered genius.

From my balcony, I had a bird's-eye view, of course, of the streetlight-dotted freeway—a pulsing artery and lifeline for hardworking New Mexicans. The streetlights were like beacons of hope, guiding people to and from home at the beginning and end of each long day. It reminded me of the Yellow Brick Road that called Dorothy home from Oz. Well, I wasn't in the 'burbs anymore, Toto.

Living costs in Albuquerque were reasonable: I had ensuite laundry, Babs had her own private garage, and airport parking was only two dollars a day. This came in handy, since I found myself on a plane almost every other month.

But Isabel was right. In the end, I didn't have much waiting for me back home in terms of a romantic relationship. It had been five years since my separation, three years since my divorce, and six months since I had left Yogi Boy to use his own fuel to fill up his gas tank. So, what did I have to lose with Callum? Plus, people have tropical flings all the time, right? I mean, let's be real: I lived in America, and he lived in the jungle in Costa Rica. It's not like this would become a thing.

Right?

Wrong. It already was a thing. In fact, if you believe in the power of the planets, one could argue it had become a thing long before the two of us even met for the first time. It was clear that Callum and I had a soul contract and were destined to meet at this point in time.

As the weeks passed, we shared several meals, ocean swims, and beach sunsets together, and the spark between Callum and me was undeniable. The women in my training couldn't hold back their observations, commenting on how "cute" we were together, how we had "googly eyes" for each other, or how much "love" they felt between us already. Even Callum's eight-year-old daughter, who stayed with him every other week, asked him about the girl "with the booty" (which was eight-year-old language for "Black-Ass Bitch"). They weren't wrong. And while I kept insisting that I lived in America and he lived in the jungle, it was evident this tropical fling was definitely becoming "a thing."

Indulging in our insatiable conversation on his rooftop deck one evening, Callum and I paused to look up at the starlit night sky. Suddenly, the mood shifted, and before I knew it, Callum and his googly eyes leaned in for a kiss.

I gazed up at the clear, expansive night sky and tracked the tiny stars lining up in long constellations. Just like the streetlamps lining the Albuquerque downtown highway or the Yellow Brick Road calling Dorothy home, I already felt right at home on this rooftop deck in the middle of the Costa Rican jungle.

And then I heard it. "Here he is," the Universe whispered into my heart. "Your beloved."

What if, I thought to myself, *I am in exactly the right place, exactly where I am supposed to be?*

What if everything I had lived and experienced up until that point was so I could, indeed, end up right there on that rooftop in the jungle? What if the Universe knew that Callum and I needed to wait decades and travel halfway across the world before we could be truly ready to meet each other and fulfill our soul contract?

I closed my eyes and did something I rarely did with a man. I stayed. I stayed in my body and stayed out of proving anything. I stayed in the moment, instead of just going through the motions. I stayed grounded ready to receive, instead of drowning in self-deprecating thoughts.

Something was different. For the first time in my adult life, I felt something I had never felt before—true intimacy.

I softened into Callum's intoxicating kisses, quivered as his hands and lips slid across my skin, and sank into sultry sensations.

As a different kind of spirit animal cat purred in my lap that evening, it dawned on me that what I was feeling was the deep connection I had been searching for my entire life. Letting go of any semblance of immiguilt, I reminded myself that I was Serena fucking Arora, and I deserved this moment. As I immersed myself in the tantalizing, passionate exchange of pleasure, it came to me that this was the Universe's response to my letter. Callum was the one I had asked the Universe for. He knows who he is, he owns his place in this world, and he has lived a similar path as me. He's self-assured, humble, generous, successful, strong, sexy, and oh, was I being *ravished!*

I looked up at the twinkling oasis of the infinite Universe and mouthed the words, "Thank you," before closing my eyes and falling into euphoria.

Callum and I spent the next eleven months video calling and traveling back and forth between Costa Rica and America, spending time being and teaching together. We met each other's friends and families, and since we were both shaped from divorce, we decided to honor the process by giving each other a lot of space to navigate this newfound love.

I was wrong about tall, White, tattooed sales-y guy: Callum was the furthest thing from sales-y. He turned out to be one of the most genuine, thoughtful, integrous, articulate, perceptive people I had ever met, and I liked him a lot. More important, I liked who I was when I was with him. I felt safe, playful, vulnerable—feelings I never thought could coexist.

When I was around Callum, I felt sexy *and* smart, desired *and* deeply valued, confident *and* curious. I possessed a kind of rooted femininity when I was with him that felt new to me and yet natural at the same time. He brought out the juicy feminine side of me that was grounded in comfort and ease—the shiny side of Serena, who always lived within, waiting patiently to emerge.

There was no agenda, no proving, no grasping, and no desperation. I wasn't looking to "win" him, and Winona was nowhere to be found. I didn't believe I could feel this way in romantic partnership, but my relationship with Callum taught me otherwise.

I didn't even know this kind of vivacious feminine energy existed. It hadn't been modeled for me when I was young, and I didn't know one woman in my family who openly possessed this kind of empowered grace.

Immigrit taught me that feeling connected to my senses, to joy, and my vulnerability was wrong and a waste of time. I had been shamed into believing, if I actually enjoyed my sensuality, intimacy, pleasure, and sex, I was "dishonorable," "bad," or akin to a "whore."

For a daughter of immigrants, this shame weighs heavily, mostly because it's empirically untrue. So, unpacking this heavy load is no simple task. It takes work and a partner who is willing to shoulder some of the baggage while you unpack it. And Callum was not only wanting to be that for me, he was well equipped for the job.

Callum was a mature, sensitive man who took responsibility for himself. He didn't need to be mothered, given advice, or managed in any way. In fact, he didn't need anything from me but respect. And I trusted and respected him completely, which amplified his adoration of me—all of me. It soon became clear that we were brought together to grow, discover deep connection, and support each other in breaking our outdated relationship patterns.

Callum is a great listener and a truth teller. He's not afraid to speak directly into the heart of the matter. He will call you out when you're not aligned with integrity and has the skill to stand in the storm of it. It's not always easy to hear the truth about how your behavior affects others or a situation in general.

Most people don't have the ability to hear it, vilifying the other for *their* discomfort. Not this immigrit girl. Hearing the truth not only felt safe to me, it felt comfortable. I also respected this familiar direct, tough-love approach and, with my relationship to comfort, had the immigrit to stay in a truth tornado—even if it hurt.

The issue in my tissue, however, was my relationship to criticism. I had learned, if I dared to color outside the lines of the immigrit sandbox, I would, beyond a shadow of a doubt, come face-to-face with stiff, silent judgment and explicit criticism at the very least, and public shaming at the very worst. And since I was clearly the colorful one in our large extended family, I often found myself dog-paddling in an ocean of criticism and got used to it. Not only did I learn to expect it, I almost craved it, so I could put up the immigrit shield, let negative comments bounce off of me like popcorn, and prove how strong I was to stand and take it.

So, my work with Callum was to differentiate between deflecting criticism and receiving what was actually true. If ever there was an opportunity to "stop acting like a kid," as my friend's husband suggested, this was it. I had to learn to choose to feel empowered and emboldened by the incredible gift of hard truths Callum was offering, and grow from it, instead of feeling criticized and judged, like I did when I was growing up. I could stay in my old familiar immigrit story or I could grow up, receive it, and mature into the woman I say I am.

And while the hard truths were easier for me to hear, the mushy truths were excruciating. While I was used to being admonished, I had a very challenging time receiving appreciation, love, and compliments. And Callum had no problem showering me with all three. In fact, the guy complimented me more times in a week than I had been complimented my entire life.

With immigrit, compliments were virtually non-existent. In Asian culture, it was expected that a child be respectful, dutiful, grateful, and amenable, without accolades or participation ribbons awarded for this customary behavior. So, as long as you followed the rules and ticked the boxes on the acceptable immigrit checklist, you wouldn't be criticized. And sometimes, you'd be praised, but never to your face. You'd accidentally hear about the "great" thing you'd accomplished from some distant cousin or neighbor, instead.

Receiving compliments was so foreign to me, I didn't know what to do with them. They made me feel uncomfortable at best and tortured at worst.

And since comfort and safety were the goal, I would deflect, dismiss, and reject compliments like a ninja dodging a throwing star. I was so starved of compliments, they would just bounce off me like torrential rain on parched land. I simply wasn't able to receive them.

To protect my fragile ego, I demonized compliments. I labeled them fake, overused, and, well, sales-y. And since I'd decided I wasn't deserving of them, nobody else was, either. Not only was I not used to receiving compliments, I didn't have practice giving them, either. So, I stuck with what I was comfortable with—genuine, honest criticism.

But Callum was different from anybody I had ever been in relationship with, romantic or otherwise, and I soon learned, if I chose it, our relationship held the key to my sacred treasure chest for growth and maturity. He respected me, himself, and our relationship too much to let me get away with my old, protective, critical immigrit ways. In fact, Callum triggered a kind of familiar discomfort in me that I didn't quite understand yet, but would learn to appreciate beyond measure.

Callum and I taught with, contended with, and loved with each other well. Our respect for each other continued to grow until, one evening, on that same fateful driveway in Costa Rica, Callum asked me if I'd be interested in moving in together.

I laughed out loud and blurted out, "Um, who moves to a third-world country on purpose?" I had long ago given up my teenage desire to live in Costa Rica. I liked the amenities of the developed world and appreciated so many things about living in America—including millions of people who were interested in learning more about quinoa, spirulina, and yoga.

A stunned Callum stared at me. I quickly realized I was staring back at the answer to my insensitive (and duly inaccurate) question. I guess what I'd meant was that both my parents had taken risks and left their respective developing countries in order to give me a better life, along with the birthright to a developed country with ample opportunities and privileges. I was the result of the classic immigrant story, so why on Earth would I give up a life of abundance, convenience, and uninterrupted electricity on purpose?

"We could do some cool shit together," Callum responded, matter-of-factly.

What he was saying was true. I also didn't want to make a hasty decision.

"Look," I said, "I'm on the monogamy train. So, if I move out here, that's it. Are you ready for that?"

We both agreed to keep the conversation going.

I left Callum in the jungle for now and went back to my busy life, leading yoga and Ayurveda trainings in America, Costa Rica, Hawaii, and Mexico. My network, teaching repertoire, and delivery were growing significantly, and I was buzzing with excitement for what was yet to come.

A few months later, at the Mexico City airport, while waiting for my flight back to Albuquerque, I called Callum. I was lit up about the Ayurveda workshop I had facilitated to a crowded room, and he shared in my celebration, with compliments flowing my way.

This time, I was ready for it. In fact, I was starting to get used to Callum's effusive appreciation. Although challenging at first, Callum gave me ample opportunity to practice receiving compliments, which proved to be gratifying for both of us. He told me how much he appreciated me and how he admired the work I was doing in the world, helping so many people who were hungry for what I had to offer. What I wasn't ready for was what he said next.

"I'm ready to be in an exclusive relationship with you. In fact, I'd be crazy not to. You're incredible, and I can't risk letting you go. I want to build a nest for us here in Costa Rica." He was heartfelt and vulnerable.

And yet, even with his sincere outpouring of emotion and adoration for me, I still couldn't help but wonder if moving to the middle of the jungle was the right move for me. I was standing in the airport of the most populated country in North America, a continent where more people were interested in yoga and Ayurveda than anywhere I had ever lived or visited, even India. At what seemed the peak of my career, was I ready to leave this side of North America?

Was I ready to live in a developing country and risk disappointing my immigrant parents, essentially revoking everything they had fought so hard for? Was I willing to live in a small town on the way to nowhere again?

I liked Callum. I even loved him. But was I ready to leave my currently electrifying life for the dark silence of the jungle? After all, it wasn't called Casa Sombria for nothing.

My thoughts were interrupted by my plane boarding announcement. I thanked Callum for his vulnerability, told him I'd consider what he had said, hung up, and jumped up to board my plane.

***

Back at my downtown Albuquerque loft, I set my bowl of spaghetti on the coffee table in front of me. Spaghetti is my go-to comfort food when I get back from a trip and don't have any fresh groceries in the house. I just grab a container of homemade sauce from the freezer and a chunk of parmesan cheese from the fridge, and my tastebuds are off to Naples!

I slid open my large patio doors and stepped out onto my balcony then leaned over the railing to take in the view and breathe in the city. I adored traveling, and yet there was just something about coming home. But *was* this home for me? I had lived in nine different places in only five years, after leaving my home in Deer Lake. Even then, after pouring my heart and soul into that house on the lake, did it ever really feel like home to me?

As I watched the stream of rush-hour traffic leave the downtown core and head to their homes, I wondered if this exotic bird would ever find a nest that she could truly call home. I sighed and went back inside.

Plunking myself down onto the loveseat, I stared at the freeway through the patio doors as though it were a big-screen TV filling my entire wall. I cracked some black pepper, shaved some more parmesan over my spaghetti, and took a bite. Closing my eyes, I inhaled the rich, comforting, Italian party in my mouth and chewed slowly.

My one-person party was interrupted by a low, booming roar coming from outside. I opened my eyes to see the leaves trembling on some nearby trees outside. Just then, the roar turned into the familiar chopping sound I had come to know well since moving downtown. The chops cut through the air like cleavers, and, out of nowhere, a police helicopter appeared outside my window. It streaked past my balcony toward one of the apartment complexes downtown.

Taking my spaghetti with me, not fazed in the least, I got up from the loveseat to get a closer look at the action. As I peered out my window, I couldn't see much except for the chopper's bright spotlight. Mindlessly taking another bite of spaghetti as though watching a live episode of *Breaking Bad*, I strained to hear the muffled voices in the distance.

Just then, I stopped chewing, set my fork down, and swallowed hard. *What am I doing?* I thought to myself. Here I was, an independent exotic bird, eating spaghetti all alone in my expensive nest, watching *Breaking Bad* from my window, normalizing someone else's painful reality as entertainment. Ayurveda believes you become your environment, so what on earth was I becoming?

What was I doing here, when I could be waking up at 5:00 in the morning to the sound of howler monkeys and macaws, instead of the cafe's rumbling exhaust fan? When I could be eating dinner watching beach sunsets instead of live episodes of *Breaking Bad* outside my window? When I could be surrounded by moonlight and sounds of nature instead of police-chopper spotlights and gunshots, *er*, cars backfiring?

It had been eighteen months since my CVS parking lot realization. I had worked hard to reclaim my juiciness and zest for life, and Callum and I had been dating for a year. I had a rewarding career, traveling and working in incredible places. And I had an adoring, devoted man waiting in the jungle to jump on the monogamy train together. As I felt my pattern of overwhelm looming over me like a police helicopter, I realized I wasn't coming home every month. I was coming back to a hollow space that, no matter what, would never feel like home.

I was a tropical flower, so didn't it make sense to transplant myself to a magical, tropical country that had left footprints on my fourteen-year-old heart?

I grabbed my phone and called Callum.

"Hellooo, sexy!" he chimed gleefully on the other end.

"Okay," I said, "let's do some cool shit together."

He let out an exhilarating laugh, half delighted, half relieved, and, now that I know him, I'm pretty sure he shed a tear or two.

After hanging up with Callum, I dialed my parents' number. My mom answered.

SERENA ARORA

"Oh, hey, Mom," I started. "In case you were wondering, I'm moving to Costa Rica."

Chapter 17

YOU CAN'T ALWAYS GET WHAT YOU WANT

TWO YEARS INTO MY big move to Costa Rica, I stood, fuming in the kitchen of Callum's two-bedroom upstairs suite in the jungle, and stared at him and his daughter, incredulous.

I spun around on one heel, grabbed my car keys off the table, and barked, "I've had enough of this. I'm outta here!" In full "when in doubt, get the fuck out" mode, I stormed past them, burst through the door, fled down the wooden stairs in twos, and leapt into Momo, my jungle Jeep.

I peeled out of the driveway, dust flying behind me, with no destination, just the need to go. With my windows shut and radio turned up as loud as it could go, I screamed at the top of my lungs. I charged past houses, stray dogs, and a troupe of monkeys, spewing a string of expletives that I'm sure even the animals could understand. As I bounced along the bumpy gravel sideroad, I was likely the most exciting hot mess those monkeys had seen all day in that small, lackadaisical surf town.

I had tears streaming down my face, while the blame game played on repeat in my head. *Build a nest? Ha! Yah, sure! It's a nest all right—a wasp's nest! I don't need this bullshit! Fuck this, I'm so done!*

I turned down another gravel sideroad and pressed down hard on the accelerator, pushing Momo forward like a race car, my heart pounding along with the engine. With the radio blaring full blast from Momo's speakers and tears blurring my vision, I could barely see the narrowing in the road ahead of me, where a bridge had washed out due to the copious amounts of tropical rain that we had gotten that month. And then, Momo started fishtailing.

Shiiiiitttt! I gripped the wheel harder, but I could feel the car slipping, losing control. I fought for a split-second, until somehow, by some miracle, I regained control. Steering into the skid, I brought Momo to a slow, shaking halt right at the edge of the river bank. At that moment, everything I was angry about seemed insignificant.

As my heart hammered in my chest, I could barely breathe. Trying to calm my racing pulse as though it would keep Momo steady as she teetered on the edge of disaster, immiguilt started to seep in. I dropped my forehead onto the steering wheel from pure exhaustion.

Moving in with Callum in Costa Rica was not what I'd thought it would be. And for a moment, just a moment, I allowed myself to feel it all—the frustration, the fighting, the failure. And then, the radio, still blaring in the background, captured my attention.

Mick Jagger's voice was screaming as though directly at me. *"You can't always get what you waaant..."*

I lifted my head and caught a glimpse of the weary woman in the rearview mirror.

"You can't always get what you waaant. But if you try sometimes, well, you just might find, you get what you neeeed..."

Mick Jagger's recognizable howl cut through me like a full-moon-ceremony machete.

The woman in the mirror—tired, angry, worn out, resentful. A mess. And it was my mess.

"Frick, Serena," the voice in my head kicked in as I turned the radio off. "How the hell did you let this happen *again*?"

The words hit me with a ruthless sting, cutting through the silence of the car.

The voice got louder. I couldn't escape it. "You're halfway across the world for fuck's sake! What the hell is it going to take for you to stop this?

"Oh, I know. How about this? How about you just stop?

"Stop pointing the finger. Stop blaming others. Stop running.

"You can't always get what you want, and guess what? You got exactly what you asked for! You asked for this, remember? Different country, different road, different car, same lofty expectations."

Ouch. When it came to scolding (especially myself), I was the queen... Or the Rolling Stones, in this case. Did I, once again, layer my high Asian expectations of success and efficiency onto the lackadaisical Pura Vida (simple Costa Rican) lifestyle? And right there, in the aftermath of that realization, perched on the edge of a riverbank in the Costa Rican jungle, I sat. I sat in the stillness of another near-accident. I sat with myself. It's true, wherever you go, there you are. The message had finally broken through, loud and clear. I can't always get what I want. I got what I need.

Moving to Costa Rica didn't end up being an easy-breezy walk into the beach sunset. Before leaving my downtown Albuquerque loft, I set an intention for my move—to slow down, connect with nature, and streamline work projects. Before I made the move, I told Callum what I needed for that to happen. Three things: reliable WiFi, a quiet workspace, and a private space for us. However, upon arrival, I quickly realized *space* was the last thing Callum's tiny home had. And it became more obvious every day that I wasn't going to be getting some anytime soon.

Since Callum's house was directly adjacent to Casa Sombria, it was dubbed "the office." Therefore, the entire house was a buzzing beehive of activity, where staff came and went. Volunteers circled around the kitchen island for their meeting at 6:00 every morning. And, of course, Callum's daughter stayed with us every other week in the small two-bedroom, one-bathroom upper suite. Not only that, but Callum's parents were also visiting—for three months! A tiny tidbit he had failed to mention to me before I got there. Tight quarters indeed.

Needless to say, I didn't have a space to work without getting distracted, there were consistent power outages, which meant no reliable WiFi, and because Callum's parents were staying in the second bedroom, his daughter slept in ours, so no private space for us. Let's just say the nest was crowded and feathers were ruffled.

Despite it all, this exotic bird was still a great nester. Knowing what wasn't readily available in Costa Rica, I had brought down an array of substantial creature comforts with me—an Instant Pot, a Vitamix, oversized Mason jars filled with Ayurvedic herbs and Indian spices, a large cast-iron pan, and even a Dyson vacuum. When I nested, I nested hard.

And while Callum appreciated the thoughtful gesture, his daughter unequivocally did not. Not only did she not appreciate I had paid extra for oversized baggage just so I could make life easier and more comfortable for everybody, she didn't like the fact that I was there at all.

I like kids. And they like me. In fact, I like kids so much, I had surrounded myself with them my entire life. I was a kids' day camp leader at only fourteen years old, a preschool speech pathologist at nineteen, a middle school teacher and coach since I was twenty-one, a yoga teacher to toddlers and teens, a youth group-home director, and auntie extraordinaire. I didn't not have kids of my own because I didn't like them. I didn't have kids because, having worked with hundreds of kids every single day, I figured, well, why only give to two kids when I can give to two hundred? Plus, that way, I get to go to a quiet home at night.

As a result of being around kids since I was one myself, I had a comprehensive toolbox full of lessons, games, crafts, activities, and stories up my sleeve. I drew from my deep well of intuition and creativity, including a pseudo-Mrs. Doubtfire accent, to keep the kids engaged and make menial tasks seem fun. I was a natural at engaging with kids, and they seemed naturally drawn to me, too.

Except this kid.

Actually, to be fair, Callum's then-eight-year-old daughter and I hit it off at first. Whenever she said, "I'm bored," it was music to my creative ears. I'd source whatever was lying around, and we'd craft paper-bag puppets together then put on a show for her dad. I taught her the songs to my favorite musicals, printed positive affirmations and hung them on her bedroom wall, and we played games like charades, Mexican Train, and Heads Up together. We'd laugh at silly "girl stuff" that her dad didn't catch, and we baked and cooked together in the kitchen, too.

In fact, she loved my cooking and would say things like, "Smells good!" or, "Yess! My favorite!" when she walked through the door. And since making food for others is one of my love languages, my ego's belly was full, too.

However, all of this was short-lived. A year later, once she turned nine, everything changed. She didn't understand why I was still there, and she was navigating loyalty binds while managing a lot of change. Meanwhile, my ego was about to starve and die a slow and painful death.

Callum's daughter was a bright, observant, and bristly daddy's girl who wasn't afraid to show her disdain for something or someone. She had no problem telling grown men what to do and how to do it, so when it came to little ol' me, she pulled out all the stops.

One hand on her hip, the other waving in front of her face, she declared out loud, "No girl is gonna get in between me and my dad!" Unfortunately for me, she proceeded to make good on her declaration.

She would push me off benches so she could sit next to her dad. She'd rip my hand from his so she could claim it. She'd barge in on me in the bathroom after all of twenty-eight seconds (I timed it once), because I was "taking too long," I'd be interrupted as soon as I opened my mouth, if Callum and I dared to have a conversation with each other.

I'd be told to get into the backseat as she sat firm, arms crossed, in shotgun (the passenger seat). I'd be kicked under tables and thrown death stares from across them. I was informed which items in the house were mine and which were her dad's (including the house itself). I got scolded for washing the pile of dirty laundry in her hamper the week she wasn't with us. I'd be woken up in the middle of night as she dragged her dad out of our bed and into hers.

And I'd end up cooking her "favorite meal," but eating it by myself after getting a turned-up nose and a request for her dad to make her something else. Which he did. (They might as well both have sent a dagger through my heart with that last one.)

I started to shrink myself more and more, feeling small. Defeated. Disappointed.

Attempting to discuss any of this with Callum only made things worse; it was the one topic that drove a wedge between us every time. He was protective of her, felt guilty, and decided she and I would have to work out our differences on our own.

I was used to working things out on my own. What I wasn't used to, however, was being a "stepmom." Nobody I knew had a stepmom, and none of my close friends or family members were even divorced, let alone stepmoms. So, for me, this was completely foreign territory—the deepest culture chasm yet. I had naïvely thought, with all my experience with kids, it couldn't be that hard. These famous last beliefs, along with immiguilt, led me to fail miserably at stepmotherhood.

I also learned (the hard way) that parenting advice from first-family moms is completely irrelevant to second-family stepmoms. The same rules simply do not apply. So, when I turned to Google for help, I really had no idea what I was looking for. I hadn't even identified myself as "stepmom," until I needed something to type into the search engine. After being woken up in the middle of the night by Callum's daughter yet again, instead of going back to sleep, I lay in bed, ruminating and searching for answers in the abyss.

It was one thing being an outsider, coming into someone else's home, and having to navigate a new living situation. But the close-knit, attached-at-the-hip (literally) relationship that Callum had with his daughter took my predicament to a whole other level.

Both tall and lanky, Callum and his daughter often walked arm in arm, hip to hip, their long legs propelling them far off into the distance, while I trailed behind them like a puppy dog. They ate together, slept together, whispered together, and loved each other fiercely. Callum doted over her, was at her beck and call, and treated her like a princess. She protected him, jumped to his defense, and followed him around like she was his bodyguard.

After taking several trips away alone to clear my head and reset, I was often met upon my return with mixed emotions and haughty updates from Callum's daughter. She'd proudly report, "I slept with Dad the entire time you were gone."

While my immigrit wouldn't allow me to relate to this type of parent-child relationship and discipline (or lack thereof, in my immiguilty opinion), I also found their dynamic quite exclusive, ostracizing, and even humiliating at times. Their relationship left no room for anyone else, and sometimes I wondered why I was even there at all.

Their dynamic triggered in me the very familiar feeling of being an outsider and a recurring character in yet again another episode of *Sesame Street's*, "One of these things is not like the other" segment. Not only that, but being in a second family triggered my second-place wounds—the familiar trap Serena fucking Arora had worked so hard not to fall into again. And a position I certainly never expected I'd be in with Callum. And yet, here I was, smack-dab in second place.

It doesn't matter if you're being called a Paki, a whore, or a city slicker in a small town, the feeling when you're different, when you know your presence isn't appreciated and you're not welcome, is damaging to anyone's soul. Callum's daughter made it very clear I was not welcome in the space, so for me, this was the ultimate test. Was it possible for my soul not to belong, yet still emerge undamaged? Only time would tell.

Those first two years living in Costa Rica, I went from fully engaging and enjoying being with Callum's daughter to pretty much avoiding her at all costs. I'd prepare myself for the now ten-year-old's attitude storm as she sauntered through the door every other week by steadying myself for the inevitable blame coming my way for whatever had or hadn't happened in the house while she was gone.

I'd get ready to shield myself from the contemptuous glares, snide remarks, and bossy commands: apparently my blender was too loud, I used my blow dryer too early in the morning, I left the shower handle set to a temperature that was too high, and the list went on and on. I found myself walking on eggshells and, while I had indeed slowed down, connected with nature, and pared down my workload, I must admit, I felt more comfortable watching helicopter police raids from my downtown loft in Albuquerque.

I felt like one of those punching bag clowns with the weighted base. Punch. Bounce back. Punch again. Bounce back. Punch harder. And, because I loved this little girl's father, instead of going down for the count, I sucked it up, painted on a smile, and bounced back—immigrit.

Things were decidedly different in the house whenever Callum's daughter was around, but the stress of those weeks, amassed over two years, had a ripple effect through our relationship. After our first two years living together, compliments from Callum became fewer and further between, and things between us grew decidedly tense. My emotional tug-of-war combined with Callum's self-afflicted DDGS (Divorced Daddy Guilt Syndrome—I swear it's a thing) left me feeling confused, rejected, exhausted, and completely alone.

I started to sleep less and less. One night, I woke up and realized I hadn't slept through a full night in two years, not since moving to Costa Rica. Partly because I'd get woken up by Callum's daughter coming into the room, but also because I was teeming with resentment. My nervous system had been on overdrive, and the anxiety and stress grew so bad, I ended up with a full-blown autoimmune disorder.

The classic signs and symptoms of rheumatoid arthritis ravaged my hands. I could barely open and close them, and the pain was excruciating. I was a seasoned yoga therapist and Ayurvedic health practitioner and only forty-four, but I was dropping glasses and dishes, I needed help opening jars and lifting heavy pots and pans, and my deformed knuckles looked like gnarled tree roots or the hands of a ninety-year-old arthritic woman. My life, my love, and now my health were all being run by a disgruntled ten-year-old girl, at this point.

Something needed to change, and fast.

No matter what it took, I needed to send that little girl to the back of the bus, with all the other ten-year-olds, and get my grown black-ass bitch back into the driver's seat of my own life. Even if it meant firmly gripping the steering wheel with my deformed hands.

Being a stepmom was by far the most challenging role I had ever taken on, which meant moving to Costa Rica was one of the hardest moves I had ever made—and that says a lot, considering how many times I've moved.

I started to question my decision almost every day, and I wanted to leave more times than I could count. Was this worth it? There are eight billion people in the world, so why him? I never wanted to have children in this lifetime, so why her? I was single, no kids, self-sufficient, and in the prime of my life, so why this?

And so, I made it my mission to understand the lesson behind my situation and dissect it in as many ways as I possibly could, with the help of people who understood—immigrit.

A straight-shooting stepmom coach and stepmom, herself, Mary T. Kelly said that there is no greater, more selfless role than being a stepmom. In an interview, she was describing the role of a stepmom. When asked, "Is there anything *good* about being a stepmom?" she chuckled and replied, "Well, if you're into personal growth, there's nothing else like it."

Ah. Growth.

In business terms, since the initial return on investment of being a stepmom is dismal, one can only consider it a long-term investment for growth. In practical terms, my immigrit convinced me that I was made to do hard things, all in the name of growth. In spiritual terms, the Universe apparently only gives you what you can handle, and in times of darkness, I'd often hear, "You asked for this, remember?" In my yogi uncle's terms, *being* yoga is the manifestation of growth. In Mick Jagger's terms, you can't always get what you want, you get what you need to grow. And in my own terms, I knew in my heart this would be my biggest growth lesson to date, and Callum's daughter would be my greatest teacher. As I mentioned earlier, my relationship with Callum was a match for us both to grow. Unbeknownst to me, it would be his daughter who pushed me to find my edge.

The truth hit me hard, like a sudden gust of wind knocking me (and my car, Momo) off balance. And the truth was that I was jealous. I was consumed by it—the unshakable bond between Callum and his daughter. It wasn't just a father-daughter connection. It was something deeper, something sacred. He spoke to her with a patience I never knew growing up. He listened in a way that made her feel seen, understood—something I never experienced as a little girl. He never raised his voice. Never shamed her. Never blamed her. No matter what she said, didn't say, did or didn't do, she was free to be herself with him at any given moment, and he accepted her fully just as she was. No matter what. That was a level of parenting I couldn't even fathom.

Their bond—so pure, so strong—was a constant reminder that I would never experience that kind of connection with my own father. And there, in that pain, was the crux of it.

The way she was so secure in his love and his unwavering belief in her—it reminded me of what I had never had. Nor ever would. I wanted to appreciate their bond, and yet, at the same time, it burned me. That, no matter how hard I tried, no matter how much I yearned for the gap between my dad and me to close, I had to accept the painful truth: it wouldn't.

The culture chasm between an immigrant parent and their diaspora child simply does not allow for this level of intimacy. To be that vulnerable goes against every traditional moral and cultural fiber of the very fabric from which immigrit and immiguilt is spun. I couldn't escape it. Not in this lifetime. Simply put, the little girl in me was jealous of the little girl in front of me.

And so, I had a choice. I could lament the fact that this kind of father-daughter relationship wasn't in the cards for me in this lifetime, or I could choose to celebrate the little girl whose karma it was to receive this rare level of respect and intimacy with her father in hers.

I get it. Callum's daughter wasn't angry at me; she was angry at the situation. She didn't hate me; she hated what I represented. I had her dad's attention, something she wasn't used to sharing, and her young brain believed I was replacing her. She thought his loving me meant he would love her less. She couldn't process her emotions on her own and, since I wasn't her parent, I was the perfect target for her to project her frustration onto. I get it.

What I didn't get was how well she treated other adults in her life. So, I started to assess why she showed certain people in her circle respect. What I noticed was that all those people held firm disciplinary boundaries. I, on the other hand, in my sad attempt to win(ona) her over, had abandoned my boundaries and given away my power. She was able to blame me only because I allowed myself to be the easiest person to blame.

She was my real-life Winona, who did whatever she needed to do to win at all costs. And I had allowed her to jump straight into the driver's seat of my bus! I felt demoralized once again, playing it small and settling into the comfort of second place—the backseat. And so, I turned to the only thing that I knew I still had left in me—immigrit.

So, in 2019, during that third year living in Costa Rica, I channeled my immigrit to rebuild strong, unwavering boundaries with her, with Callum, and with myself. I sourced Ayurvedic herbs, food, and rituals to reduce the inflammation in my body. I transformed the bedroom closet into an ensuite bathroom, reclaiming an eggshell-less sacred space where I could be free to move (and pee) as I pleased. And I joined online groups for stepmoms and women, where I finally came to realize I wasn't crazy or a terrible person after all. More important, I wasn't alone. Operation self-care was in full swing.

The truth was that this girl was in my life to unveil my deepest core pattern and teach me the hardest lesson to date—to be the mother I never had. Children look to their mom to be seen just as they are. And just like I was a tropical flower, they also emerge as the flower they actually are. Whether as a lily, tulip, or cactus rose, they're also hoping they'll receive a nurturing toward who they are, not some arbitrary picture of who they ought to be or based upon some standard of what their parents never were.

My parents didn't understand what my tropical flower-self needed in order to thrive, and for decades, neither did I. So, if I truly wanted to break the immiguilt pattern of conditioning, I had figure out what kind of flower Callum's daughter was and give her something I'd never had—empathy.

So, I chose to be grateful for having this feisty now eleven-year-old girl in my life, who mirrored my own behaviors at times and taught me more about myself than any other person ever could. I chose to be grateful for getting exactly what I'd asked the Universe for, four years prior—Callum. And I chose to be grateful that I had enough courage, grit, and grace to live, honor, and grow from it.

I do believe the Universe only gives you what you can handle. In my case, it took an immune disorder, an ego death, and more near-miss car accidents than I'm proud to admit in order for me to see where I needed to change. You can put an Asian girl in the jungle, and she may or may not survive, but if she does, it's because she learned (the hard way) to let her demanding Asian expectations go, so she could let simple jungle life in—pura vida.

And to all the stepmoms and brave women out there who might be contemplating stepmomdom, know that it's not for the faint of heart. You're not alone, you can't always get what you want, and you most certainly will get what you need. Thanks, Mick.

Chapter 18
SECOND MARRIAGE PROPOSAL

AS PART OF MY ONGOING self-care practice, I needed to take breaks from jungle life every so often, so I would visit my family in Canada, while Callum held down the Casa Sombria fort in Costa Rica. Now that my parents were in their early eighties, I made a point of visiting them more often and for longer periods of time. I also liked staying there because, unlike our Costa Rican treehouse, I had my own spacious basement bedroom, bathroom, and living room all to myself. Plus, I figured it was also good for Callum and his daughter to have their own time and space together, without me around. Win-win.

In April 2019, I had just returned from the gym when I decided to call Callum and say good morning. Going to the gym had been a staple for me since I was eighteen. My first group fitness class in university was so impactful, I became a fitness instructor at age nineteen. I had prioritized going to the gym at least four to five times a week for decades.

Until I moved to Costa Rica, that is. We lived in the jungle, and the closest gym was forty-five minutes away—one way! So, without a car when I first arrived, I stopped working out literally overnight. I'm quite certain my body went into shock. And I no longer had a healthy outlet for my stress.

Therefore, the taxing family dynamic between me, Callum, and his daughter, combined with no gym, had exacerbated my arthritis symptoms. I know this because the symptoms would subside as soon as I left the jungle. It became clear that walking on eggshells, not taking up space, and living in a state of fight-or-flight was taking a severe toll on my physical, mental, and emotional state. With that, I took as many opportunities as I could to leave the jungle. I traveled to the U.S. and Canada for work and to visit friends and family often. Once there, I could resume my endorphin-producing workouts, reclaim my own stress-free living space, and eat familiar food that my body craved.

Ah, food.

With my family being half Indian and half Chinese, our entire social structure revolves around food. It's no surprise it has become one of my love languages then. Making food for others brings me great joy, and eating delicious food made lovingly by others has also been an indulgent self-love practice that I've carried into adulthood. When it comes to food, I gravitate toward the Indian side of my plate. My Chinese mom learned to cook Indian food from my Indian rebel uncle when she first got married, so we grew up on mostly Indian food, with smatterings of Western food from recipes my mom cut out of the newspaper. Indian food felt like a familiar hug to my body, and my digestion and elimination always seemed to do better after a few days of eating simple, savory Indian meals.

When I lived in Costa Rica, however, it was difficult to obtain the ingredients for cooking Indian food, and my body missed the authentic flavors, spices, and comforts that reminded me of home. And, well, you know my relationship to comfort. So, whenever I came back to Canada, I took advantage of a home-cooked Indian meal to nourish my body and feed my soul.

While chatting with Callum on the phone, I looked around the bedroom, eyeing the neatly folded piles of clothes that lay on the bed and the half-packed suitcase sitting on the floor. Callum and I were planning to meet up in New York City in just a few days for a networking conference and to celebrate his birthday, before going our separate ways again.

"Okay, you smart, sexy, brown beauty, I'll see you soon!" he signed off in his typical cascade of compliments as we hung up the phone.

I went upstairs to make myself some breakfast. As I paused at the top of the staircase, I saw my mom slowly unloading the dishwasher. With a recent Parkinson's diagnosis, she seemed to find systematic tasks like unloading the dishwasher comforting, even therapeutic, and she had grasped onto it—literally and metaphorically—before having to eventually give it up entirely.

"Morning, Mom," I called out.

"Oh, hi, Serena. I thought you had gone to the gym," she crooned with her back toward me, setting a teacup in its rightful place in the cupboard.

"I'm back now," I replied, explaining the sequence of events so she could track my whereabouts in her slowly fading memory bank.

I walked into the kitchen and peered into my parents' fridge. As I searched for something to eat, my mom and I circled around our usual conversation starters—the gym, the weather, the breakfast options. I grabbed a stack of stuffed parathas and a tub of plain yogurt. My dad was the paratha maker in the family. His stuffed parathas, layers of flatbread filled with any combination of cooked onions, cauliflower, and potatoes, were always a special weekend treat when I was growing up.

Now, this tradition has been passed down to my niece and nephew, whose mixed-race palates have an appreciation for international flavors and diverse cuisine. Having inherited our food love language, my dad's parathas are on the top of his grandchildren's list, not only because they're tasty, but mostly because they're made with love.

I hummed my way around the kitchen, sourcing mango pickles and other Indian condiments to eat with my stuffed paratha, while I heated up the tava, an Indian cast iron pan.

My dad appeared from around the corner and sang out, "Morning, beta."

"Morning, Dad." I replied.

Though in their eighties, both my parents are highly lucid, mobile, and could pass for a decade younger than they are, but my dad is especially spry for his old age. There are long-life genes on both sides of my family, but my Indian side lives especially long and healthy lives. Most of my aunties, uncles, and first cousins look perpetually thirty years younger than their age and have lived well into their nineties and hundreds. I had always attributed this longevity to the Indian diet, and after studying Ayurveda's food-as-medicine approach, I'm now convinced of it.

My dad prepared his usual breakfast, an elaborate hybrid concoction of grains, almonds, cashews, turmeric, cinnamon, ginger, cardamom, maca, and raw honey from a local honey farm. He'd buy gallons of honey, and neighbors, friends, and family needn't guess what their birthday or holiday gift from my dad would be. Instead of shoes lining the steps leading down to the basement of my childhood home, in this house it was a cluster of three-to-five-gallon honey pails—a virtual obstacle course I had to maneuver every evening before going to bed.

My dad went to the front door, propped it open, and bent down to grab the rolled-up newspaper from the stoop. His morning routine consisted of sitting down to his hot bowl of cooked goodness and the daily news.

After a few minutes, mid-chew, he turned to me and said, "Soooo, what are your intentions with Callum?"

I furrowed my brow and jarred my head back in response to my dad's random question.

If there was one topic I never spoke about with my traditional Indian dad, it was my love life. And if I ever made the mistake of mentioning anything about it to my mom, it would almost always come back to haunt me, when she brought it up again in front of my dad. (You'd think I would have learned my lesson the first time, with my breast buds.)

However, I have a soft spot for sharing things with my mom. We often took long walks, and I would tell her all about my personal life. Partly as a feminine-bonding moment, but mostly in an attempt to find relatability, nurturing, and understanding. While that rarely happened, I still love talking to my mom because she's a good listener (and I'm a good talker). However, I almost always have to brace myself for the opinionated judgmental remarks, the unsolicited advice, and then the uncomfortable silence that ensued.

Hearing my mom's opinion, especially about my love life, rarely felt supportive to me and often left me doubting myself even more.

I realize now that this communication dynamic between us was the Universe's way of giving me ample opportunity to practice working through my relationship to discomfort. However, when it came to discussing my romantic relationships with my mom, I had to prepare myself well in advance to fight in the war zone of shame, disloyalty, and dishonor. Let's just say there were many casualties (mostly from my side) and the war, er, conversation, never ended well for me.

In fact, the only time I voluntarily sat my parents down to speak about the status of my romantic partnership was when I was getting divorced. I prepared myself for what I believed was going to be a mature conversation between the thirty-eight-year-old adult me and my parents. I told them that the split was amicable, the best decision for us, and to not to see it as a failure.

My dad's reaction proved otherwise. He held his breath while I was speaking, made the disgust face—the crinkled nose and brow, like he had smelled something bad—then interrupted my prepared speech by raising his fist and shouting, "You don't think a failed marriage is a failure? It is a *failure!*" He slammed his fist down on the table.

I instantly melted into a puddle of shame, the devirginized sixteen-year-old teenager, kneeling on the kitchen floor again. Failure was the F word in Asian culture. And since relationships in general haven't ever been very easy for me, talking about my personal life with my parents almost always felt like a big, fat swear word to me. So, I divulged information on a need-to-know basis, and they never pried.

Until now.

"What do you mean, 'my intentions with Callum?'" I stammered, scrunching up my face in an attempt to hide my discomfort.

"I mean, what kind of relationship do you people have?" he replied.

My dad used the term "you people" often, but I never really knew exactly what he meant by it. He sometimes used "you people" to refer to Westerners or even White people. Sometimes, he used "you people" to refer to females. Sometimes he used "you people" to refer to us kids of immigrants. And, while the references differed, the meaning almost always alluded to the same thing: that he did not relate to us, understand us, or agree with us. He'd growl, "You people!" followed by some accusatory remark with his disgust face, then swiped the air between us with his backhand for good measure.

It was his go-to phrase whenever he felt offended, judged, invalidated, criticized, or if someone just had a different opinion from him. And because I adopted those same insecurities, I heard "you people" often. For me, hearing my dad say "you people" immediately put me on the defensive. It triggered the protector in me. I quickly put on my boxing gloves and jumped into the ring to make sure he wouldn't hurt that little girl in Buster Brown shoes again. It sparked in me the same anxious uncertainty I'd had when waiting for my name to be called over in an old-school game of Red Rover. You know that game where you left the safety of "your" wall to plunge headfirst into the dangerous depths of "you people" on the other side?

Except, this time, when my dad called Callum and me "you people," it felt different.

Instead of feeling defensive, I felt proud to be partners on the same team and side as Callum—a united front.

Callum and I had been together, and committed to each other, for four years at this point. And while our relationship had its challenges, he was undeniably my person. Sure, it hadn't been easy, but growth is messy, and we both had a strong desire to work through the mess together. Callum and I were on the same team. We were "you people" on the same Red Rover wall, and, admittedly, I loved the man.

So, I answered my dad with as much candor as the daughter of an immigrant father could muster. "We're in a committed relationship," I stated emphatically.

My dad continued his line of questioning. "What would you say if he asked you to marry him?"

"I'd say yes," I answered without hesitation.

Whoa. Wait. What had just happened? Did I just say that out loud? Did I just have an honest, mature, adult conversation about my romantic relationship with my Indian dad? Did I just answer his question with conviction, like I did with people who weren't my parents? And did I just divulge my romantic feelings about someone without fearing judgment or feeling immiguilty?

For a very brief moment, the shadow of an elusive bridge between my dad and me appeared in the culture chasm.

And then "Poof!" it disappeared.

The bridge crumbled into obscurity when my dad started his next sentence with the word "taxes." My vulnerable declaration of love was dismissed by this turn to "tax talk." The bridge dissolved into the abyss below, and the culture chasm was immediately restored—ah, immigrit.

I was accustomed to "tax talk." Accustomed to ignoring it, that is. My dad was a corporate controller, my sister Vice-President in Assets & Finance, and my mom's second career was opening and operating her own private tax preparation company. Needless to say, tax talk was everywhere—at the dinner table, in the car, on the phone, and now, after proclaiming my love over a hot bowl of breakfast cereal.

As my dad went on, talking about other non-matters of the heart, my mind shifted to the idea of my actually feeling ready to get married again. I really thought getting married again was the furthest thing from my mind. But when I heard the confidence of my answer, the "I'd say yes" come out of my mouth, it was apparent that it came from my heart.

For the first time in my life, I felt proud to proclaim my love and commitment for someone else. I felt aligned, congruent, and unwavering in my response. Whenever I spoke about my relationship with Callum, it felt like it was coming from a much deeper place in my body. Like the girls at the full-moon ceremony, it came from the depths of my heart, my gut, and my womb. It was a full-body "yes." It was aligned truth.

As my dad wrapped up his tax-talk monologue, he offered me a final piece of unsolicited advice for good measure.

"Okay, don't get married. Just stay committed."

Pondering yet another confusing culture chasm convo with my dad, I let out a heavy lukewarm sigh and sat down to eat my now equally lukewarm parathas.

***

Callum and I were reunited a few days later. As we held hands on the New York City subway, we chatted about the things we had planned for that week: the conference, visiting some old friends, Times Square, and a professional photoshoot. Photoshoots were an important part of the marketing landscape in our business, so I figured some shots of us in the Big Apple were in order.

It was a chilly spring afternoon for our photoshoot, with a chance of rain. A former student and friend of ours tagged along, acting as another set of eyes—were our arms too high? Hips too low? Messy hair? That sort of thing.

After two hours, the streets were wet, and Callum and I had been running around in bare feet. As we struck our last pose—headstand—in the middle of a busy intersection in Manhattan, it started to drizzle. *Perfect timing,* I thought to myself, feeling a bit chilled and looking forward to getting inside somewhere warm.

But Callum convinced the photographer to take one last picture. *What? One last picture? In the rain?* And we'd just done a headstand... I worried *what was my hair like now?*

However, since everybody else seemed game, I followed suit. And, heck, why not? We were in New York City, baby! As the photographer directed us in front of yet another narrow Manhattan street, I asked Callum what pose he was thinking of. He didn't answer right away.

Again, I probed, "What pose are we doing?"

"Turn around and face that building," he replied, pointing behind me.

As I turned to face the building, I thought, *Aw man, I hope it's not a backbend... My backbends are seriously questionable these days.* I stood there for a brief moment, contemplating my backbends, before Callum told me to turn around. *Phew!* I thought as I turned around. *No backbends.*

No backbends indeed. But there was Callum on bended knee.

As he tearfully professed his love and adoration for me, along with his desire for me to be his wife, I stood there, speechless. With both hands over my fallen open mouth, a hush rolled through me. All I could hear was the thumping of my heartbeat and then a tiny voice from behind my right shoulder. My dad's voice echoed, "Don't get married. Just stay committed."

C'mon! I screamed on the inside. *Not this again!* Not another, "Are you sure?" moment after a marriage proposal!

Just then, I heard our friend's voice from behind the photographer to my left. "Say yes!" she yelled.

And, like a classic cartoon skit, the angel and devil appeared on my shoulders and started "should-ing" all over me.

"Just stay committed."
"Say yes!"
"Just stay committed."
"Say yes!"
Stop!

I closed my eyes, ground my bare feet down into the Manhattan asphalt, and dropped into the soft, quiet, undistracted place in my heart, my gut, and my womb. And there it was, the answer I was looking for. The aligned truth.

I gazed down into the tearful googly eyes of the strong, mature, sensitive man whom I was proud to love and who loved me back fiercely. The person I had asked the Universe for, my beloved. The man I had waited years for and traveled oceans to meet. A man who jumped on the monogamy train with me, ready for the ride. A man who loved everything about me, from my shit-brown eyes down to my black-ass bitch. A man who had the courage to *claim* me.

I took a deep breath and, with the pure, honest, unfiltered innocence of a four-year-old girl holding her Buster Brown shoebox, stood proudly with outstretched arms and shouted an emphatic, full-body "*YES!*"

***

I found out later that my dad's line of questioning wasn't random at all. Callum had written to my parents, asking for their permission to marry me. After this chivalrous gesture, they gave him their blessing, and I got, well, tax talk.

Now that I had just accepted a second marriage proposal, I started to become curious why I'd thought marriage wasn't a top priority for me. I mean, let's face it, marriage hadn't gone that well for me the first time around. Maybe, just maybe, if I put some thought into it, the result would be more favorable this time. Plus, there must have been a reason why the Universe afforded me a second chance, right?

Actually, everything about my relationship with Callum felt like a second chance, a mulligan of sorts. And I was hellbent on not repeating my same relationship pattern with Callum. I didn't want to maintain a lackadaisical long-distance dynamic with my romantic partner again. And I certainly didn't want to experience another divorce. I was getting another chance to learn from my mistakes, to make different choices, and ideally to have a different outcome. So, if I wanted a different result, I had to figure out the common denominator in all of this and then change it.

That common denominator was me.

So, I looked inward. I looked at myself, dissected my patterns of behavior, and discovered what I did and didn't do to contribute to the demise of my relationships.

I tracked it back all the way to that Buster Brown moment, when I was punished for expressing myself so fully. I dimmed my light and decided I was bad, guilty, and wrong about something. When I found out that I had been misunderstood, I proceeded to do whatever it took to win and prove that I'd been right.

How this shows up in my adult romantic relationships is that I show love by expressing myself honestly. Sometimes too honestly. Meant to be helpful, my honest feedback can come across as harsh, critical, and judgmental, instead. Due to my unskilled delivery, the other person feels offended, and I feel misunderstood. I would then defend myself in an attempt to prove that my intention was pure. As a result, conflict ensued. Then, fearing the worst, I would leave. Worse still, I didn't even have to leave physically to leave the conversation mentally. When in doubt, get the fuck out.

Leaving is my way of creating distance and space between us, which is something I learned from my parents. If one kept their distance long enough without communicating or apologizing after conflict, the space would somehow magically erase what had occurred and everything would go back to normal again—immigrit.

Space and distance were also often masked as independence and non-jealous behavior by me. However, I extended the long, liberal leash so far and wide between us, we found ourselves floundering out in space, disconnected and lost. And when left out there for too long, the space would inevitably be filled with something or someone else—which complicated and burdened the relationship and eventually ended it altogether.

It took me a while to realize that the distance I kept between my romantic partner and me was not because I wasn't jealous. It was my strategy for avoiding conflict at all costs. I had carelessly created this space with my lack of boundaries and poor communication, leaving my partner wondering, wavering, and confused. And the message was that they were irrelevant and didn't matter. My mask of hyper-independence actually hid my genuine commitment, availability, and reliability. Eventually, the person on the other end of the rope no longer trusted that I needed or even wanted them.

Meant to give space to the relationship, the leash had, in fact, ended up strangling and suffocating the relationship itself. Ironic. And it wasn't until the leash came whipping back, hitting me upside my divorced head, that I woke up to the fact that my approach was indeed flawed. It had bred a level of separation, emotional unavailability, and betrayal that neither of us could recover from. I then used the leash to swing all the way to the other side of the jealousy pendulum, where I clutched, mothered, and smothered a high-desert hyena so hard, karma forced me to loosen my grip.

You see, there are two sides to a jealousy coin: owning and claiming. While nobody can actually own another person, there exists a primal desire to be desired, needed, and *claimed*. My hyper-independence and immigrit, which I had inherited, didn't allow for me to be claimed because my emotionally immature mind confused being claimed with being controlled. Since I avoided being controlled like the plague, I therefore never made myself available to be claimed. And if I ever got close (i.e., marriage), my reaction was to let the leash out a little bit longer. It was a highly effective strategy... to push people away.

Yoga is often translated as union. And if yoga is indeed the closest thing to human nature, then separation in and of itself goes against human nature. While I craved union in my relationships, my immigrit reminded me that there was always a "you people" on the other side. So, by strategically placing myself on the opposite side from my partners, at the end of the Red Rover game, I found myself all alone on one wall, because my partner had given up attempting to call me over.

And by not claiming them, they were available to be "claimed" by someone else.

So, if I didn't want to relive this pattern in my relationship with Callum, I had to claim him just as he had claimed me. I had to change my perspective on marriage and, more important, partnership. I had to stop seeing partnership as unnecessary, insignificant, or an accessory to my life. Instead, I needed to value it with the honor and respect it deserves.

I had to toss immigrit to the curb, break learned relationship patterns, and hold myself accountable. I had to practice validating, communicating, and appreciating the effort it takes to sustain a quality and elevated partnership. I had to replace independence with interdependence and reacting with receiving. I had to place myself on the same Red Rover wall as my partner and trust that we'd face "you people" together as a team. And I had to reclaim the grounded feminine wisdom that lived in the depths of my heart, gut, and womb.

And I needed Callum to know that he mattered, and not only was he relevant in the relationship, our relationship was a priority. I was ready! However, the Universe had other ideas.

Just as I was preparing to fly back to Costa Rica and put my newly awakened feminine grace to the test with Callum and his daughter, a global coronavirus pandemic broke out. Borders closed, planes were grounded, and I stayed put. Clearly the Universe felt I had more to explore with my relationship to space and distance, and that I had more work to do. Alone.

So, this exotic bird smoothed out her newly acquired feminine feathers and settled back into her parents' basement nest and got to work on herself... for the next ten months.

Chapter 19
HONEY, I'M HOME

"OKAY, YOU HAVE everything you need?" I asked Callum's daughter as I quickly jumped into the driver's seat of his car.

Toting her horse-riding boots and gear under her arm, she clambered into the passenger's seat. "Yep!" she replied enthusiastically.

After the pandemic, I was back in the saddle, so-to-speak, as I chauffeured her to her riding lesson that morning.

As we pulled out of the driveway, I glanced over at her. She had turned twelve that year and become a young lady while I was away. Taller than me now, she had decidedly grown into a more mature version of herself, both physically and energetically. As she stared out the passenger side window, I noticed we were sitting side-by-side, facing the same direction for what felt like the first time. I couldn't shake the feeling that, perhaps for once, we might just be on the same team, too.

Steering to dodge potholes, dogs, and randomly stopping vehicles, I also acknowledged that I was indeed back in the driver's seat of my life and calling the shots. As part of my work to claim my relationship with Callum and his daughter, I asserted myself firmly in the role of partner, stepmom, and the mother bird of the nest. I also claimed responsibility for my own health by unapologetically taking up the space I needed in order to thrive, while attempting to include others in creating a comfortable nest for us all. With that, I was in the driver's seat, and Callum's daughter was exactly where she wanted to be all along: riding shotgun.

After ten long months apart during the pandemic, Callum's daughter and I got reacquainted on the short drive to the barn. We chatted about school, her recent birthday, and horse competitions. She seemed different. Receptive, open, and generous with her answers, and she seemed genuinely happy to see me.

After a slight pause, I turned to her and said with a kind smile, "You've changed."

"Yeah. That's what all my friends' parents have been telling me, too." she said without missing a beat, still staring out the window.

"Why do you think that is?" I probed.

Without taking her eyes away from the side window, she paused as though contemplating a thoughtful answer before turning toward me.

"Well, I guess, a while ago, I was at my friend's place, and I heard her bossing around her parents and some of the house helpers. I didn't like how it sounded—kinda bratty and... well, like me. I talked to people like that, too. So, I decided to stop," she explained with a simple twelve-year-old's matter-of-factness.

I stared at her, stunned by her newfound maturity and accountability for her behavior.

"Wow. Most adults don't even reflect on, or own, their behavior like that. I'm so proud of you!" I gushed.

Keen to give me another example, she brought up a trip we had taken together a couple of years ago—one I had vowed to never take with her again. Calling herself out, she admitted sheepishly, "Yeah... I was being a real brat on that trip."

I couldn't believe what I was hearing. Perhaps both of us had grown up that year. Callum's daughter seemed more settled, accepting, and might even have missed me a little bit. I had generated a powerful Ayurvedic self-care practice that reversed my rheumatoid arthritis and honed my feminine energy. And with no guests or significant other to tend to, our time apart had also afforded Callum an opportunity to focus on himself—something he rarely gets to do. It was clear that a lot was about to change in our little jungle nest.

After dropping Callum's daughter off at the barn, I headed back to the house and, now that I was back in Mother Nature's epicenter, started thinking about my role in the nest and my relationship to motherhood. I had spent the last year learning about healthy feminine behavior, and I was determined to model it in the space and with the people I felt the most challenged by. I knew, in order to do that, I had to focus on taking responsibility for two intricately connected things: my reaction and my self-care.

Not only could I control those two things, I realized they ultimately determined the mood of the entire nest. In my experience, the way a woman builds and maintains her nest is directly dependent on how secure she feels in her own skin. A nest can feel safe or stressful, comforting or controlling, mothering or smothering. And, if mama bird isn't securely grounded in herself, the entire nest can feel fragile, unstable, and even upend, because the ripple effect of the feminine force is undeniable. With just one word, a look, or a particular tone from the feminine, the rest of the nestlings can feel shielded or scared, delighted or dismissed, nurtured or neglected.

Thus, in order to provide a comfortable nest in which everyone can thrive, having a solid self-care practice is essential. And as a result of mothering myself in this loving way, I was able to become more present not only for myself, but also for moments with Callum and his daughter.

Generating greater understanding, deeper compassion, and broader empathy brought Callum and me closer together, and compliments started flowing my way again. It was only with this level of presence and care that I could, indeed, as Callum said, do some cool shit together. Together, we transformed Casa Sombria into a bright lighthouse in the middle of the dark jungle—a streetlamp-lined highway guiding people from all over the world back home to themselves.

Before the pandemic, in order to avoid ruffling anybody's feathers, I had let my self-care practice go by the wayside. I felt so depleted that, rather than laying beautifully vital eggs, this exotic bird could only manage to walk carefully on its empty eggshells. I was too weak to break through when I was called over in a game of Red Rover and, in the end, was no help to anybody, especially myself. This self-abandonment showed up as reactive, dysregulated, and disconnected—unhealthy feminine behavior that disempowered mama and all her nestlings. So, not only did it affect me, it affected Callum and his daughter, too. It dismantled the safety of the nest, also impeding their ability to grow and fly—the very purpose of a nest to begin with. This showed me firsthand how unselfish a daily self-care practice really is.

The feminine is, in its essence, a self-care practice. It teaches us at a young age what it means to foster community, nurture family, and sustain life itself. She has the capacity to either hold a family tapestry together or snip it apart piece by piece, until there's nothing left of it or of herself. The power that the matriarch holds is immeasurable and has shaped our perspectives and practices around humanity for centuries, weaving a magical feminine collective thread through the generational fabric of grandmothers, mothers, and daughters.

I also acknowledge how much our mothers, our grandmothers, and their mothers have suffered. For centuries, they have had to endure a longstanding fight just to have the right to stand fearlessly in their own feminine expression. And whether we want to admit it or not, we've all been affected by it. Because, how can a weary woman give that which she does not already possess herself?

She can't.

And thus, true feminine power remains tired and untapped, generation after generation.

My mom is one of those weary women who was born during the Second World War, a time when food was rationed, pecking orders were formed, and decisions were ruled by fear and worry. (It's no mistake the words worry and fear together make "weary.")

In traditional Chinese culture, at the beginning of the twentieth century, feminine beauty was determined by the size of a woman's feet. Keeping her feet small and dainty in the name of beauty was the cruel justification for breaking and binding a girl's feet at a young age. Since this limited her mobility, ability, and independence, it hampered her feminine power and kept her submissive to, and dependent on, her male counterpart.

My great-grandmother fell victim to this egregious tradition; however, when it was my grandmother's turn, her fierce courage and desire for freedom saved her from experiencing the same debilitating fate as her mom.

My grandmother, bravely refusing to follow tradition, used her unbound feet to run away from home right into the safe arms of my grandfather. Together, they left Canton and made a life for themselves and their little family in Malaysia and Singapore. Then, as fate would have it, they followed their adult children to Canada.

My grandmother passed down her bold, relentless need for freedom to her daughter. And her daughter passed it down to me. We are a long line of small women who have the ability to stand up for themselves, even in the face of life's biggest challenges. However, this desire to fly the nest was born out of a wobbly undercurrent of fear, with our unbound feet walking on eggshells with trepidation. And so, disguised as freedom, my grandmother carried this burdensome torch of fear with her across the globe. She passed it down to her daughter, who, in turn, passed it down to her daughter, little Girl Arora.

Lineage is powerful. In her childhood, my mom didn't feel loved by her own mother. By not being mothered in the way she needed to be, my mom deeply believed that she was unlovable.

Love was such an unfamiliar and uncomfortable concept for my mom that, although she deeply craved it, she also avoided it at all costs. She believed she was undeserving of love and never knew what love sounded, tasted, or felt like, until she met my dad.

And even then, she pushed it (and him) away, afraid of what she didn't know or perhaps even scared she might lose it at any moment, which would be even more painful. And so, like me, she kept a long, protective leash between herself and everyone else, including her own children and grandchildren.

Our capacity to love is based on our mother's capacity to love, which was based on her mother's, and so on. And while we all have mothers, very few of us have actually been mothered in the way we needed to be. While I knew that I was loved, I still craved a more nurturing kind of comfort. I desired a level of emotional safety and support as well as physical intimacy that my mother, herself, did not receive.

My mom showed us love the only way she knew how. Tough love. She kept us "safe" through limiting, advising, instructing, nitpicking, criticizing, and building walls. She warned us not to take risks, to expect too much, or to live too largely, too loudly, or too proudly. I learned to lower my expectations of myself so I wouldn't experience failure. I learned to ignore my need for validation in case I'd never get it (like her). And I learned to view criticism as care, stoicism as strength, and opinion as truth. I call it *femmigrit*.

Navigating emotions, acknowledging them, and giving them a voice were all distant concepts in our culture and tradition. My mother could not connect with my emotions because she was disconnected from her own. She couldn't have vulnerable conversations with me because it felt like a foreign language to her. And she couldn't hold space for my big-ness because she denied taking up space and owning her own tiny place in the world. She simply could not give to me what she, herself, did not have, and I was left to navigate my emotions on my own.

My mother's deep insecurity shaped her relationship to trust, intimacy and nurturing. It disconnected her from her heart, so she not only rejected receiving love, she withheld saying, "I love you," to anyone for decades. And while grandmotherhood softened my mom, it wasn't enough to eradicate the self-deprecating internal narrative that tormented her well into her senior years, manifesting as disease.

I inherited the same disconnected, independent feminine force that kept me and others small, "safe" (afraid), smothered, controlled, dominated, and judged— *femmigrit*. And because I didn't have children of my own to pass the femmigrit torch down to, I projected its sharp flame onto my intimate partners and myself, instead. My mom's narrow narrative became my own inner critic, external judge, and fearful decision maker.

Winona was my mother. And her mother. And her mother.

Winona's voice in my head mirrored my mother's fear and lack of self-love, which manifested as my own self-abandonment.

I walked in the shoes of many generations of bound-footed women before me. These weary women were well-versed in repressed feelings, physical and emotional abandonment, and misinformed decisions. While they all did their best with the resources they had, they also made choices from oppressed minds, hearts, guts, and feet.

I, too, feared missteps in relationships and life, walking on the fragile eggshells in my nest. I dropped to my knees like a deflated clown, allowing life's inevitable upsets to easily bowl me over. I also pushed away love, criticized out of care, and demeaned out of doubt. I had an equally challenging time articulating appreciation, compassion, and love. As a product of tough love, I lacked the skill to stand firmly on my own two unbound-yet-bound feet. And so, I developed wings instead.

My wings were born from Buster Brown fear, driven by immigrit, and clipped by Winona's failed attempts to keep me safe. Just like the women before me, I used my self-made wings to flee from fear, pain, and the uncomfortable grips of love, searching for a more comfortable nest to land in. I, too, had become a hyper-independent, willfully blind, and painfully indecisive young woman who was sorely disconnected from her deepest needs, wants, and desires.

From the moment I was born, alone in the incubator, Girl Arora longed to nestle into the warm bosom of her mother's open-hearted, nurturing, feminine wings. But I never received that kind of love. So, I spent my entire life searching for it in all the wrong places and then pushing it away when it did come my way. Independence became Girl Arora's name, and immigrit was her game.

It wasn't until I was walking with my eighty-one-year-old mother one day that I realized I had literally followed in her tiny, size-four footsteps. I realized, even though my larger size-six, more privileged feet walked with a resilient, independent, and gritty gait, they still held a generational fear that kept me off balance and on guard.

I finally understood I had used my unbound feet to run away from past experiences that weren't even mine. And the discomfort of the bunions that plagued my mom's eighty-one-year-old feet was waiting for me, too, if I didn't break step, change directions, and find a different path to walk. If I was going to walk my own path with the secure feminine confidence and true grace that lived within, I had to break this demoralizing matriarchal pattern.

My mom was able to give to her children that which she did not receive from her mother, until she had nothing left to give. Thus, even though I didn't have children of my own, it was my responsibility to unpack this burdensome load from the shoulders of weary women, and stop this torch from scorching the next generation. It was my daughter-duty.

With each step I took while on that walk with my mom, I made a silent promise to little Girl Arora. From now on, I'd plant my two unbound feet firmly on the ground and stand for her, no matter what. I'd unapologetically take up space, tap into my intuition, and nestle her to my breast whenever she needed.

So, I did the conscious, courageous work to reparent myself. To shake off the fear, fluff up my feathers, and build a warm, nurturing nest *within* me—the place I had searched for outside of myself my entire life. No more winning first or second place. I'd make decisions that aligned with the truth of my heart, my gut, and my womb.

I forgave Winona, my mother, and her mother. I repeated the affirmation, *"I accept her for who she is, not for who I wish she had been for me,"* until it coursed through my blood lines and sank into the lineage of my bones, all the way down to my unbound feet. I took little Serena in her Buster Brown shoes under my wing, whispering, "I love you" to her softly every day. I committed to a sacred self-care practice, welcoming my teenage self back home to herself every night. I even announced my arrival out loud every time I entered the jungle nest.

Each time I neared and crossed the threshold to the upstairs suite in the jungle, I'd shout out loud and proud, "Honey, I'm home!"

At first, Callum laughed at my quirky new habit. When I explained I was doing it in order to affirm my sense of belonging in our home, our relationship, and within myself, he enthusiastically replied, "Welcome home, honey!" every single time. This approach was my fearless declaration to claim myself, to provide myself with an inherent sense of belonging, and to take up space within myself and within this world. It wasn't the little town on the lake or the classroom or the cardboard box or the jungle nest where I felt trapped. I managed to shrink into the four walls I had built around me all by myself.

Perhaps the work is to stop looking outside of ourselves, stay out of the extremes, and simply continue to orient one's compass back to our own center. Dedicating myself to a daily Ayurvedic self-care practice supported me in coming back to my center. It helped me redefine my relationship to my emotional body. I explored my internal landscape every day, regenerated my inner soil, and took up fertile space within myself—the true definition of fulfillment.

I finally understood what my Chilean therapist meant by repotting my tropical-flower self. Only by getting to know what kind of flower I was could I then see what made me wilt and what I needed in order to feel alive. I needed to cultivate a nourishing internal environment in which my exotic self could bloom. Immigrit taught me to survive, but the deep self-love I created internally allowed me to thrive.

By reconnecting to the innermost parts of my being, I was reminded that my sensuality and sexuality were not a shameful liability but an essential gateway to awaken my body's resilience and capacity to receive. By feeling more, I cared more, made more aligned decisions for myself, and felt more connected to others. Feeling and sensing into my body helped me tap into my womb space—where my sacred knowing and intuitive wisdom live. I felt more fluid and connected to a resilient feminine force I'd never known existed before, instead of the whore that my body believed itself to be all those years.

I had replicated my parents' stingy love dynamic in my own marriage. It took me decades, a divorce, and meeting Callum and his daughter to understand the power of the human heart. When we can recognize a need that has never been met and then give to someone something you never had, that's called redemption.

I had discovered the true essence of my beauty, the "pretty" I was told not to waste. It was a gem on my crown that, in order to shine, needed daily buffing, polishing and refining. Not only did it take years for this princess to find the crown she'd lost, it took her decades to keep it from falling off. And then years more to finally realize her immigrit would, in fact, serve as the friction needed for the precious gemstone (her) to shine brightly.

My yogi uncle's advice to "be yoga" was his attempt to guide me inward, so I could discover this precious gem for myself. *Being* yoga from now on meant that, wherever I was, I was coming home to myself.

My heart held the answers that my head would never know. My gut carried the fiery courage to put one unbound foot in front of the other. And my womb contained the wise intuition to heal and nurture myself and others, in the ways no nest outside of me ever could. My body *was* my nest. My body was my home. It always was.

It took five decades and travelling the globe in search of somewhere to call home, only to discover that my home was within me the entire time.

My body was the source of belonging that I had been searching for all along and now had managed to reclaim. Unfortunately, my mom didn't get to hers on time. Now eighty-six years old with Parkinson's and dementia, my mother can no longer write, even though her impeccable teacher's handwriting still neatly adorns masking tape and sticky notes on items all over their home. She can no longer remember current dates and times, even though she still remembers the exact day of the week she stepped foot on Canadian soil. She no longer goes for long walks and suffers from a disease that will eventually stop her tightly unbound feet in their tracks.

But I have a feeling her adventurous spirit and deep commitment to freedom will live on in her heart forever. She may still not fully love herself or even her "perfect" body, and yet stands fiercely tall at only 4'8" like nobody else I know. And in those fearful moments when she's feeling weary and defeated, I will be there for her with open, adult, feminine, nurturing wings, ready to pick her up, draw her into my bosom, and give her a warm nest in which she can feel safe, validated, and—finally—loved.

If I've learned anything from immigrit, it's that discomfort and sacrifice in one generation breed comfort and ease for the next. My parents willingly took a risk to walk through the culture chasm for the benefit of their children, their grandchildren, and their potential great-grandchildren. They tread carefully when they were met with challenge and resistance, and their hard work and determination got them through to the other side.

Because I was born when they got to the other side, I automatically inherited opportunity. I also inherited the privilege to explore my dreams, my feelings, and my relationships. Therefore, I see it as my daughter-duty to use my inherited resources to boldly build a strong, resilient bridge that connects us all.

Despite her fear, my mom had enough courage to put one tiny foot in front of the other across the culture chasm. Despite doors closing, my dad made his dream of building a safe and secure nest for all of us a reality. Despite waking up to glass walls around me, I now have the capacity to break through them and build a bridge instead. A bridge on which we all feel safe to stand, enjoying the view over the culture chasm. A bridge for all generations to look back and see how far we've come. And when the time comes for Red Rover to call my parents over one final time, they can cross over the chasm at peace, knowing we were all just "you people" on the same team.

As I drove up the long driveway, returning to our little nest in the jungle, I caught a glimpse of myself in the rearview mirror. This time, I gazed at the glowing, grounded, vibrant woman who was smiling back at me. I looked straight into her brilliant brown eyes and whispered out loud, "Welcome home, honey."

I was ready.

Ready to take up space and stand firmly rooted in my feet this time. Ready to claim aligned relationships. Ready to set a powerful example of a nurturing feminine force. Ready to show up for myself and be the woman my younger self needed. Baby Girl Arora in the incubator, little girl Serena in her Buster Brown shoes, and the lost young teenager on her knees in the kitchen—all of whom dimmed a piece of their naturally vibrant, playful, curious, expressive, quirky self in order to survive.

Accepting, welcoming, and loving all parts of me is the only way I'm able to steward the next generation of girls... with my bravely undimmed torch.

Because, in the end, we're all on our own journey, driving down Death Road. The questions are, how will we get to our very final destination at the end of this long trip, and who will we choose to bring along for the ride?

I got out of the car and confidently headed up the wooden staircase, setting one foot firmly in front of the other as though they donned brand-new chestnut-brown Buster Brown shoes. Moving with grace and ease, I turned the doorknob, swung open the front door, and boldly stood at the threshold.

With outstretched arms, in full body *yes* celebration of my newfound freedom within, I took a deep breath and proudly announced at the top of my lungs, "Honey, I'm home!"

If you're interested in learning more about Serena's offerings, or if you're looking for a guest speaker on your podcast, please visit:

www.serenaarora.com

Follow @serena_arora on Instagram

Acknowledgments

THANK YOU TO MY family for your generous support and unconditional love.

Thank you to the Hay House Editorial Team for Honorable Mention; Robin Rinaldi, Pia Edberg, and Kathryn Galán for wading through my messy drafts and believing in my message; and Samantha Joy and Raina O'Dell at Landon Hail Press, for getting me to the publishing finish line.

Thank you to Monique Giroux for being the catalyst for getting the words out of my head and onto paper; Julia Hauch, Andara Michael, Monica Arora, and Vicky Kravariotis for being a generous beta cheering squad.

Thank you to David Lipsius for holding my hand across Struggle Street and reminding me that "the only way through is through"; Chantal Gauthier-Vaillancourt for breaking the hard, incongruent truths to me gently; and Tim Thompson for everything.

Thank you to Dr. Vasant Lad for changing the trajectory of my life; Tias and Surya Little for being a thirst-quenching oasis for me in the New Mexico high desert; Tania White, Hannah Victor, and Jennifer King for keeping me intentionally sweaty and inadvertently sane; and Priya and Mohit Arora for giving me a soft place to land at a hard time in my life.

Thank you to the trailblazing women who helped shape the journey back home to myself: Claire Zammit *(Feminine Power)*, Katherine Woodward Thomas *(Conscious Uncoupling)*, Arielle Ford *(Art of Love)*, Alison Armstrong *(Understand Men)*, Giordana Toccacelli *(Embodied Feminine Wisdom)*, Meleah Manning *(Radiant Relationship Academy)*, and Brenda Ockun and Mary T. Kelly *(Stepmom Magazine)*

Thank you to all my students over the last thirty years, for being my teachers.

Thank you to each one of you who bought and read my book, for your trust and for joining this important conversation.

SERENA ARORA

About the Author

WITH HER RICH ASIAN heritage, Serena brings a lifetime of Eastern wisdom and over twenty-five years of diverse lived experience to her teaching, training, and writing. A former teacher and director for troubled youth, Serena was deeply impacted by the widespread insecurity she observed in the young women she worked with. Because she was once them.

As an Ayurvedic health practitioner and certified yoga therapist, Serena empowers women to break free from the noise of external expectations and cultivate conscious relationships—beginning with themselves. At the core of her life's work, Serena believes, when more women channel their inherited resources toward a sustainable, soul-led path, the more power they will hold to spark healing— within both themselves and the heart of humanity itself.

Born in Canada to a Chinese mother and an Indian father, Serena offers an underrepresented voice for those navigating the silent shame of the culture gap and trusts her book will be a catalyst for igniting often-unspoken conversations.

Serena now lives in the lush jungle of Costa Rica with her beloved partner, where she facilitates trainings, hosts retreats, and co-creates vibrant meals and cookbooks alongside the culinary team at their wellness retreat and spa on the Pacific Gold Coast.

www.ingramcontent.com/pod-product-compliance
Lightning Source LLC
LaVergne TN
LVHW011416080426
835512LV00005B/83